Software Engineering and Java

Software Engineering and Java

Glen K. Blood

Published 2019

Glen K. Blood
260 Villager Drive
Saint Simons Island, GA 31522

gblood@ccga.edu

1st Edition 2019

ISBN 978-0-359-89787-2

Table of Contents

About the Author

Glen K. Blood has a B.A. in Mathematics from
The Illinois Institute of Technology, a B.S. in
Meteorology from the University of Utah, and an
M.S. in Computer Science from West Chester
University. He was a Captain in the USAF, where
he fell in love with computers and the science and
art of developing Computer software. He has held
almost every role in software development
including programmer, Systems Analyst, Project
Manager, Team Lead, and Database Administrator.
His experience has included multidimensional
worldwide databases, orbital mechanics, image
processing, product quality control, and marketing.
Since his retirement from The Coca-Cola
Company, he has been an instructor in Computer
Science and Mathematics at the Coastal College of
Georgia in Brunswick, GA

Chapter 1. Software Engineering

Projects

Every project is going to have a number of factors to consider, but the big three are always"

Time
Budget
Quality

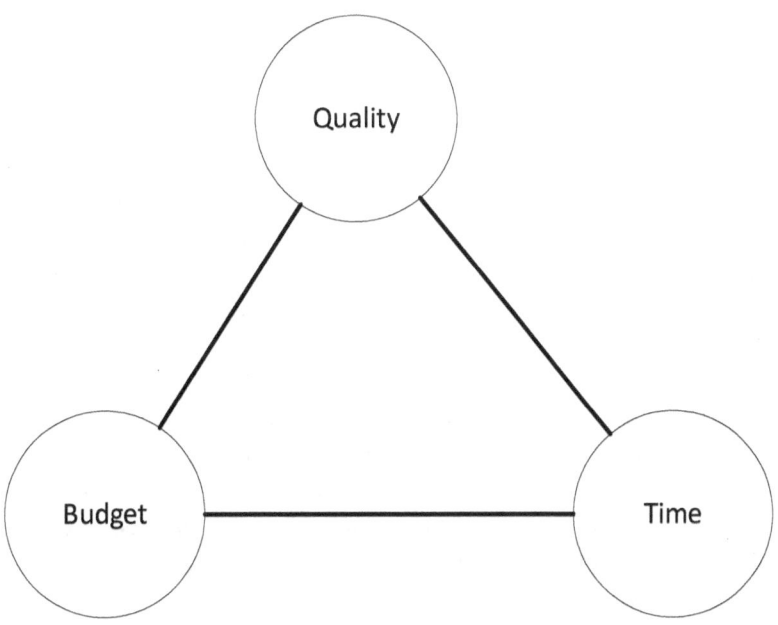

It is usually difficult to find a balance between these three critical factors and bring in a quality product on time and under budget. What does a quality product mean?

Quality Product

It must meet the requirements. What are the requirements? Like a school assignment, the requirements are those detailed items that dictate what the software must accomplish and in what way it must accomplish those items. We will get into more detail shortly.

It must contain minimal errors after the project is implemented. Errors or bugs as they are commonly known are anything that goes wrong with the program. If you have spent any time working with a computer, you have probably encountered a few, such as, your computer freezing up, or restarting suddenly are extreme examples of errors. Errors generally come in three areas:

> Programming or coding errors.
> Logic errors.
> Requirement errors

It must be maintainable. You or someone else must be able to pick up your code and read and understand it six months or a year after you write it. They must be able to fix issues or modify it to meet new requirements.

Software Development Process

Before we begin, I need to let you in on a big secret. Coding is a small part of the software development timeline. In my experience, we used to schedule no more than 25% of the time for coding. This was before we included the implementation time.

Developing software is a never-ending quest for perfection. Ever since computer software started, people have been trying to improve the software development process. In my experience, I have probably been exposed to five or six different methodologies. In my opinion, at their heart, they all are varieties of the waterfall process, so this is what I will expose you to with some slight variances.

The waterfall process recognizes that like building a skyscraper it is more expensive to fix problems or make changes the further you get into the process. For instance, it is significantly more expensive to move bathrooms from one side of the building to the other after the skyscraper is finished than while you are developing the blueprints.

There is an additional psychological factor in that people spend more effort working when a deadline is looming. So an unmonitored project looks like:

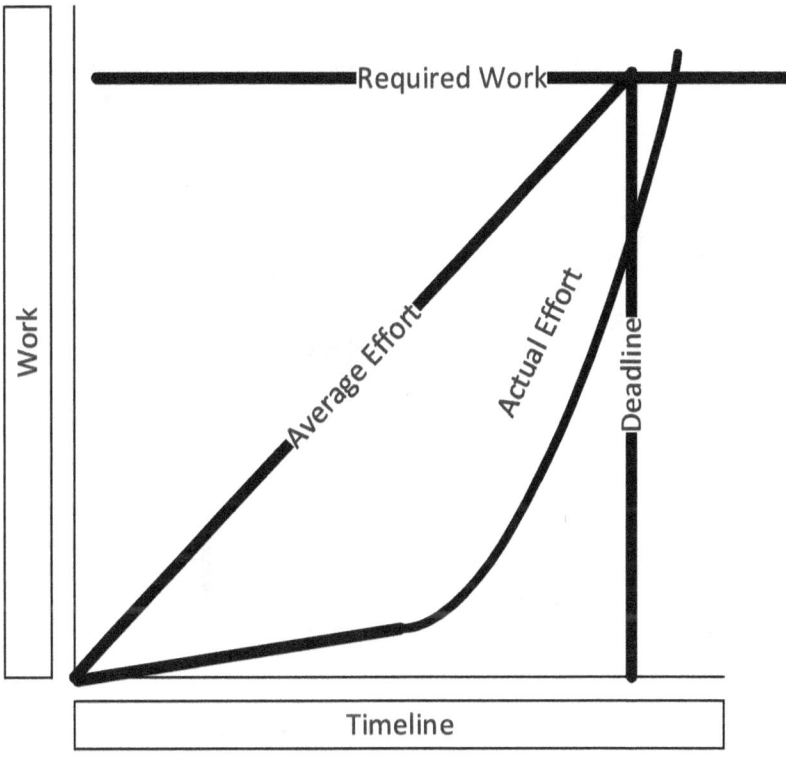

Do some of your school projects look like this? So instead of only having one deadline, the finish date, it is helpful to add reviews to make sure that measurable amounts of work are completed along the way.

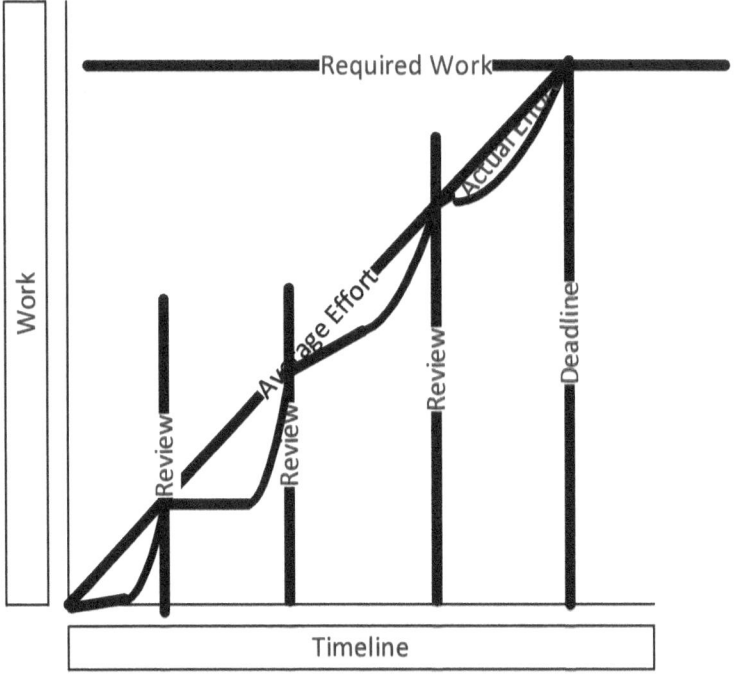

So hopefully those herculean sprint efforts are reduced, and the project gets finished on time. An additional benefit, is that by inviting customers, it gives them a comfortable feeling that work is being accomplished and they have an input into the final product.

There are some major issues with the waterfall method that other methodologies have attempted to fix:

- Customers find it hard to visualize and sign off on requirements early.
- Customers and management fail to understand that any changes to requirements will cost time and money.

8

- Customers and management perceive that for a long period of time nothing useful, e.g., software, is produced.
- Everyone wants to get to the solution early.

Waterfall Process

The Waterfall Process consists of five phases:

1. Analysis
2. Design
3. Code
4. Test
5. Implementation

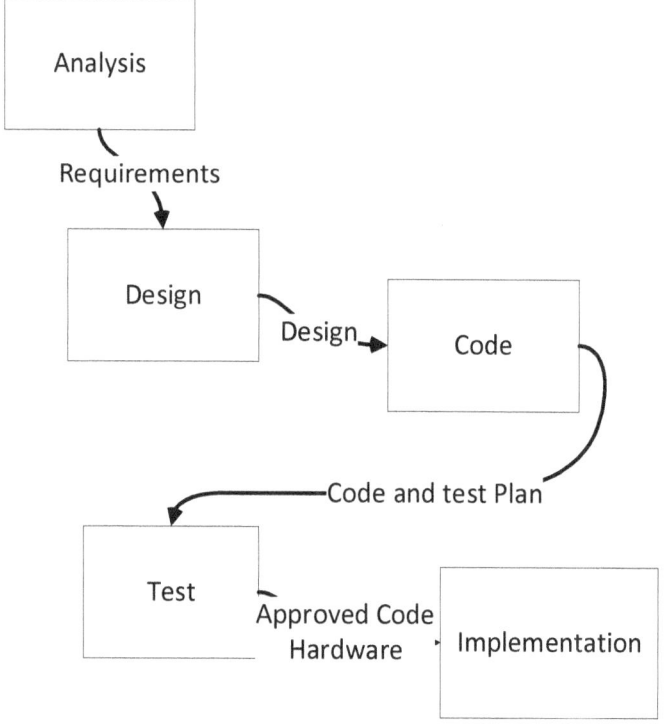

Analysis means collecting and understanding requirements. Requirements are the agreements between the customer and the development team. Requirements include everything that the software needs to accomplish. They include everything from:

- Inputs
- Outputs : Reports, Files
- Databases
- GUIs
- Business Logic
- System Requirements
- Performance Requirements
- User lists

- Security Requirements

You usually end this phase with an analysis review to get changes and a sign off on the requirements document from the customer. This should be treated as a contract between you and the customer. In some firms this is a legal document.

I quite often combine some of the preliminary design with analysis to accomplish three things:

1. Give the customer ideas for requirement definition.
2. Check requirement viability.
3. Quantify requirements.

You also sometimes build mock-ups of the GUI designs during this phase to get customer input on requirement and design options. Beware, some customers believe that the mock-ups are not throw-away code and believe that you are closer to the final product than you really are. Don't make these dog and pony shows look too good.

Design means determining the most realistic way to accomplish all of the requirements. Usually you start by breaking up the requirements into manageable sets of functionality and then designing each one separately. You might have a separate design team for each function. You then have to define an interface so that the functionalities will be able to talk to each other. The things you need to worry about are:

- Addressing as many design ideas as you can, so that you don't miss a good idea.
- Selecting a design idea that maps back to each of your requirements.
- Identifying any missing requirements. You either:
- address them in your design
- get sign off on missing requirements or
- design new functionality.
- Completing the design idea to the level that it can be coded.
- Testing the design idea to ensure that it meets the requirements.

Some of the outputs from design are:

- High level design documentation
- Low level design Documentation (code ready).
- Test cases – mapped to requirements. All testable requirements should be tested.
- Draft test plan

You probably have two design reviews during the design phase, a high-level design review and a final design review.

Code means writing the code to the design. Make certain that it is written to the design standards. Make sure that is well documented and that it compiles and runs.

You usually have a code review with either your peers and or your quality assurance (QA) section as you complete your code.

Output from this phase is usually completed code and test plans and test data.

My variation of the process combines code, unit testing, and integration testing into the same phase. Systems testing and user testing are kept as a separate phase. This is because I believe in performing code and test as I write each method as a much more effective coding methodology than just coding a large block. This has the following advantages:

- It is much easier to detect, debug and fix code in smaller chunks of code.
- It is easier (and faster) to fix issues in the last 10% of your code if you are confident that the first 90% is working.
- Even in a single module, if you code to a point, compile and test it, fix any problems, then add more code, it is faster than writing the whole thing, then trying to fix all of the problems.
- You can validate your test data early by seeing problems at a much lower level. Which is better than trying to run tests later.

There are two tools used to build/test code:

Stubs. Stubs are methods that use the same name, calling parameters, and return type as your designed method, but have no functional body. Usually, they consist of something to tell you what parameters are sent into them and return a reasonable return type. Sometimes, you can get fancy and have an internal flag variable (usually a temporary global variable) that changes the return variable to an error value. For example a stub for a method myMethod:

```
public static int myMethod(String ChangeMe){

        System.out.println(
                "inside MyMethod - ChangeMe = " + ChangeMe );
        return 0;
}//myMethod
```

Test Program. A test Program is just a small test Program that calls your method with various inputs to check it out. I usually use this method of testing when I am trying out a new coding concept and not sure how it works. If I built out myMethod and wanted to test it, I might build a driver like:

```
public class driver{
        public static void main(String[] args){
                String ChangeMe = args[0];
                int returnval;
                returnval = myMethod(Changeme);
        }
}
```

I could then run this driver against a number of valid (and invalid) values of ChangeMe to ensure that it works properly.

Test. This means testing against requirements. You or the test group follow the test plan written earlier and report any bugs which are then repaired and retested until a certain quality point (or an arbitrary date) is reached. A quality point is usually defined as a maximum percentage of bugs reported during a defined period of time. The output of this phase is the completed test report. It is usually broken out into several types of testing.

Some of these are don concurrently, although most are performed sequentially.

- Unit Testing. Testing each piece of code independently.
- Integration Testing. Joining pieces of code together and testing them together. This is usually joining individual programs together.
- Systems Testing. Testing the entire system as a whole. This usually includes hardware, software, and possibly different development teams prior to user testing.
- Performance testing. Testing normal and expected workload against any performance requirements. Examples include response time, batch processing time, wait times on database queries or page loads, etc.
- Stress Testing – Testing your system to find out when or if it will break. Increasing the number of users, or the amount of data that you input until the system breaks or until the number is so high that you would "never" exceed that limit. This is the one time that you are not unhappy to break your system as long as it doesn't break too early.
- Load Testing. This is related to performance and stress testing, except that it normally happens in a shared environment. You usually start the test system with a normal background load of other processes and then ramp up your users to test performance degradation. You usually also look at low and peak system usage trends. These usage estimates are determined by monitoring the live system, before you add your new or modified system.

- User Testing. This is testing the user interfaces with a small set of actual users from each business unit.
- Acceptance Testing. This set of tests proves to your user that your system meets his requirements. It is usually monitored by him or his representatives.

Implementation. The completed code, related data, and hardware is sent to and made operational in the field. This can be a simple or extremely complex task.

This methodology can be a complex process. However, depending on the project you can follow the process and still produce quality code in a timely manner.

Conclusion. In my experience, after you gain experience with a process, you can build quality software faster, with fewer errors than not following a process, thus meeting your requirements. And that is the goal.

Review

Meeting your customer's requirements is the actual goal of computer science. Without customers, we wouldn't have computers to play with, or any real reason to write code. You, yourselves, are customers and have almost certainly suffered at the hands of poorly developed software.

I became an early advocate for quality software development. I saw the effects of not having a good process and was taught several excellent processes. I have seen how a good process creates quality software, on time, and under budget. I have seen it, in the right hands, be flexible, and produce quality code that meets the customer's requirements in record time. On the other hand, I have also seen projects flounder and fail without a good process. Every project has three often-competing factors:

- Quality
- Time
- Budget

We attempt to meet them using a methodology. One of the oldest, that we learned about is the Waterfall, which has five phases:

1. Analysis
2. Design
3. Code
4. Test

5. Implementation

We learned that

- Analysis was all about gathering and understanding requirements
- Design was building a blueprint to satisfy requirements.
- Code is building software to the design and building the inputs for the test phase
- Test is both ensuring that your code is error free and that it meets the requirements.
- Implementation is making it available to your customers.
- By combing code and unit and integration test together in a process that I call write a little/test a little, we learned that we can reduce code errors significantly and make coding faster.

Test has several flavors including:

- Unit Testing.
- Integration Testing.
- Systems Testing.
- Performance testing.
- Load Testing.
- Stress Testing.
- User Testing.
- Acceptance Testing.

Final thoughts.

Now you may see why I said that coding is only about 25% of a projects budget. It is significant, but it is not where most of the skull sweat comes in. Don't get me wrong, I love to program. I love to see my ideas come to life, but my personal favorite part of software development is design.

I have seen a multi-million-dollar project scrapped because a high-level customer did not like a GUI design during acceptance testing. Was he involved in the requirements or design? I do not know, but that was the reason given. This is one of the reasons, I like to modularize my design and make the user interfaces separate from the business logic.

I also like to mockup the GUI and report look and feel during requirements analysis and get them signed off on as soon as possible. I may need to get changes approved later, but this is the part of the system that your customer has the most interest in.

Questions

1. Analysis is the phase in which:
   a) You design your process.
   b) You develop your code.
   c) You define your requirements.
   d) You test your code to ensure that it meets the requirements.
2. Cohesion means:
   a) How modules communicate between each other.
   b) How many things a module can do.
   c) How modules are compiled.
   d) How you set your comments.
3. Design is the phase in which:
   a) You design your process.
   b) You develop your code.
   c) You define your requirements.
   d) You test your code to ensure that it meets the requirements.
4. When writing code, it is more efficient to:
   a) Write it all, then compile and test and debug it.
   b) Write, compile, test, and debug as you go.
   c) Write the code, then send it to a friend to debug.
   d) Give up and get a new job.
5. Test is the phase in which:
   a) You design your process.
   b) You develop your code.
   c) You define your requirements.
   d) You test your code to ensure that it meets the requirements.
6. The three factors that all projects have in common are:
   a) Quality, time, and budget.
   b) Management, code, and schedule.

c) Quality, time, and code.
d) Quality, schedule, and time
e) Time, budget, and code.

7. Code is the phase in which:
   a) You design your process.
   b) You develop your code.
   c) You define your requirements.
   d) You test your code to ensure that it meets the requirements.

8. In design, when looking at ideas:
   a) Always home in on the first idea that you come up with.
   b) Always take the senior person's idea.
   c) Look for as many ideas as you can and evaluate them equally.
   d) Skip this step and code.

9. When designing test cases, which statement is false:
   a) Avoid test cases that might make your code fail.
   b) Look for outlier test cases.
   c) Use live test data.
   d) Use extreme amounts of test data.

10. When you are building your design, you should:
    a) Hide it from your customer.
    b) Show as much of it as you can to your customer.
    c) Show it to your buddies from the competition.
    d) Show it to the guy down at the corner.

Chapter 2 Compilers

We have come a long way since the first days of teaching computers how to be useful. But languages and compilers are still complicated and need to be understood. The basic parts connect to the error messages that you get when you compile a program.

When I first started programming, you would submit your entire program as a card deck to the computer operator who would then load it into the computer, and then spit out a printout with your errors. You would then painstakingly go through this printout to try to uncover every error and fix your cards. Then, resubmit your fixed cards and hope for no errors. Repeat until finished. Sometimes, it would be hours between submitting your deck and receiving your printout due to the long lines of other students doing the same thing, so you spent a lot of time on each iteration.

Now you can write your code in an editor, run the file through the compiler, get your errors, fix them, and try it again immediately. This is the real progress. This is why I advise writing part of your code, try compiling it, fix your errors, and test it. Then when you are happy with it, write some more. I call this process Write a Little, Test a Little.

The best way to understand the error messages that a compiler generates, is to understand how a compiler works. So let us have a brief discussion of compilers.

As we discussed in the introduction. Computers are stupid. They only understand zero and one.

Machine Language

The Computer Engineers that create a computer processor build in a limited set of instructions that are called **Machine Language.** Machine language consists of sets of numbers (in binary or hexadecimal) that directly reference registers, memory locations, instructions, etc. There are no letters involved. This is unique for each processor. Machine Language is executable code. In the simplest terms, processing looks like:

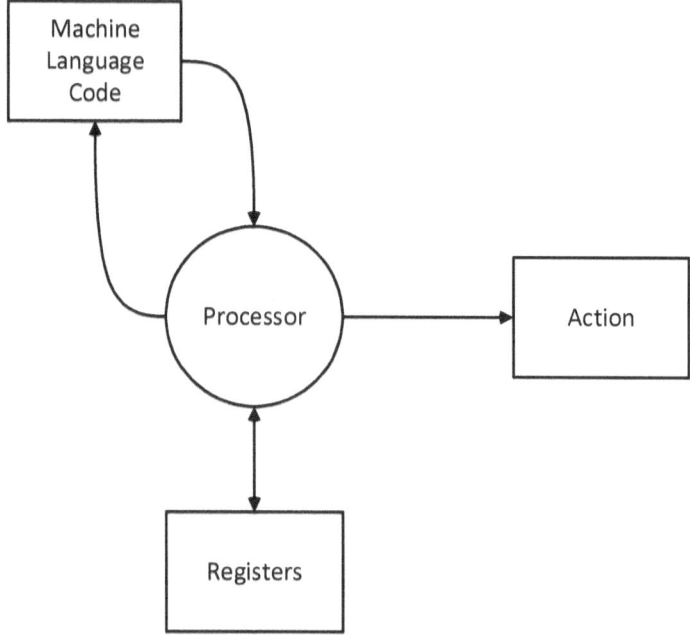

The processor gets instructions from the Machine Language Source, it interacts with its registers (very fast memory) and acts based on those instructions and goes back for more instructions.

Assembly Language

It was felt that writing machine code was too hard for humans to understand, so the next generation was called **Assembly Language**. Assembly was a little better. Assembly instructions consisted of three- or four-letter mnemonics for the instructions. Usually, registers and memory locations still had to be addressed as numbers in hexadecimal. There was usually a one-to-one correspondence between assembler instructions and the Machine language instructions. So, the Assembly language was still highly tied to the processor. You ran the assembly code through an Assembler to build the machine language (aka executable) code. This code then ran in the same fashion as described before. You still had one assembly language for each manufacturer (IBM, UNIVAC, etc.).

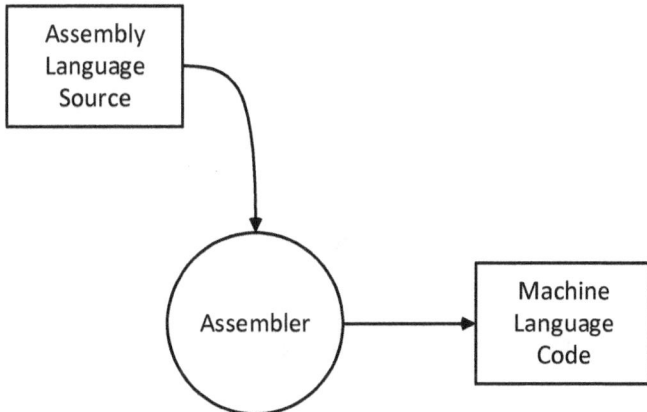

They finally got the idea that we could build languages that were almost human readable. I say almost because you still must understand the vocabulary, grammar, and syntax of the language. These languages are termed third generation. Some claim to be fourth generation, but I don't believe that any have broken out that far. Each of these languages have some form of Instructions, Variables, and Methods. They all allow you to combine many machine language instructions into one simple statement. They all shield you from worrying about registers and the inner workings of the processors. Although some will let you to get involved at that depth (for performance). This has the following benefits.

These languages tend to be transportable (to some degree) amongst systems. Unfortunately, some vendors built so many additions to languages (termed extensions) that even the source code was not transportable from one generation to the next for the same system.
These languages are much easier to maintain and modify. This does depend on the previous programmer. People can write unreadable (or as I like to call it write-once) code.

These languages generally fall into two types Compiled and Interpreted.

Compiled Languages

Compiled languages, such as C, FORTRAN, Cobol, and C++ Take the source code and run it through a compiler. The compiler takes several passes and finally (if there are no compile errors) generates executable code. You must build one compiler for each processor.

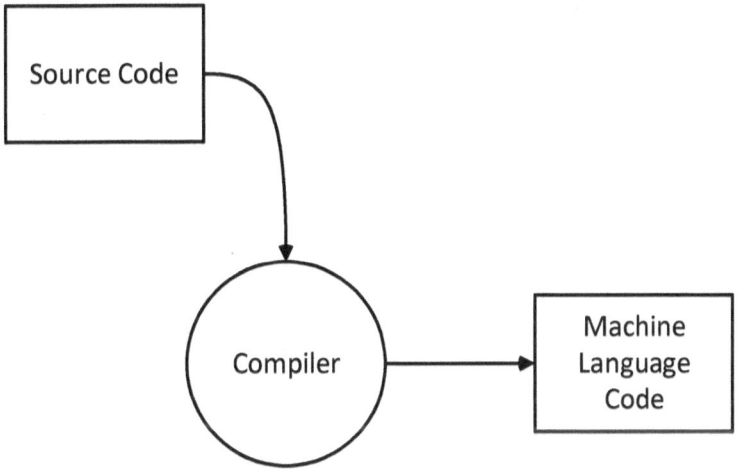

Interpreted Languages

Interpreted languages, such as Basic, Python, and R, take the source code and at run time generate the executable code. Compile errors and run-time errors are both detected at run time. This is almost (not quite) as though each line of code is turned into machine code and run immediately.

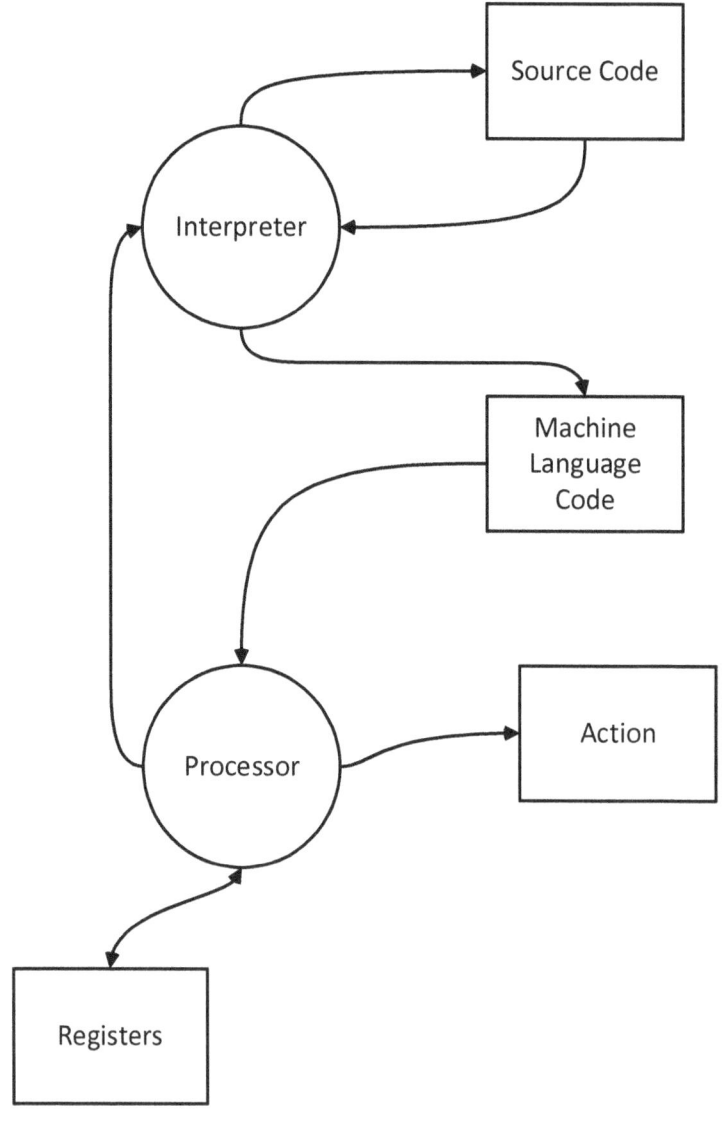

As you can see the interpreted process is very complicated and while not quite executing line by line, you can consider it to be that for simplicity.

1. The interpreter takes a line of source code.
2. Turns it into machine language.
3. Machine language is then fed to the processor for action.
4. Interpreter goes back for more source code.

Which type should you choose:

You don't really get to choose. Your language generally has one or the other.

However, the two types do have benefits and drawbacks:

What are the benefits?

Interpreters give immediate feedback and really came into use when the first micro-computers came into vogue. The systems were very small, and interpreters did not take very many resources.

Most of your Operating System command languages are interpreted.
Compilers are far better for batch processing (which is what the original computers were designed to do).

They give you an idea of more of your errors at one time. Far better, they gave you a clean bill of health (as far as compile errors) before you tried to run it.

They allow the programmer to maintain the executable code separate from the source code. So, if you are distributing your system, you only distribute the executables.

They are usually faster.

Java

What is Java? Java has a compiler (javac), but that compiler does not generate executable code. Instead it generates java binary code that you must run though the Java Interpreter (java).   I would call this a Hybrid language. This gives it the following benefits:

- Like a compiled language – most compile errors can be detected at compile time.
- The Binary File can be maintained separately from the Source code.
- The Binary File is "guaranteed" to be machine independent. So you can compile on a Windows machine and execute on a Mac.
- It should run much faster than an interpreted language.

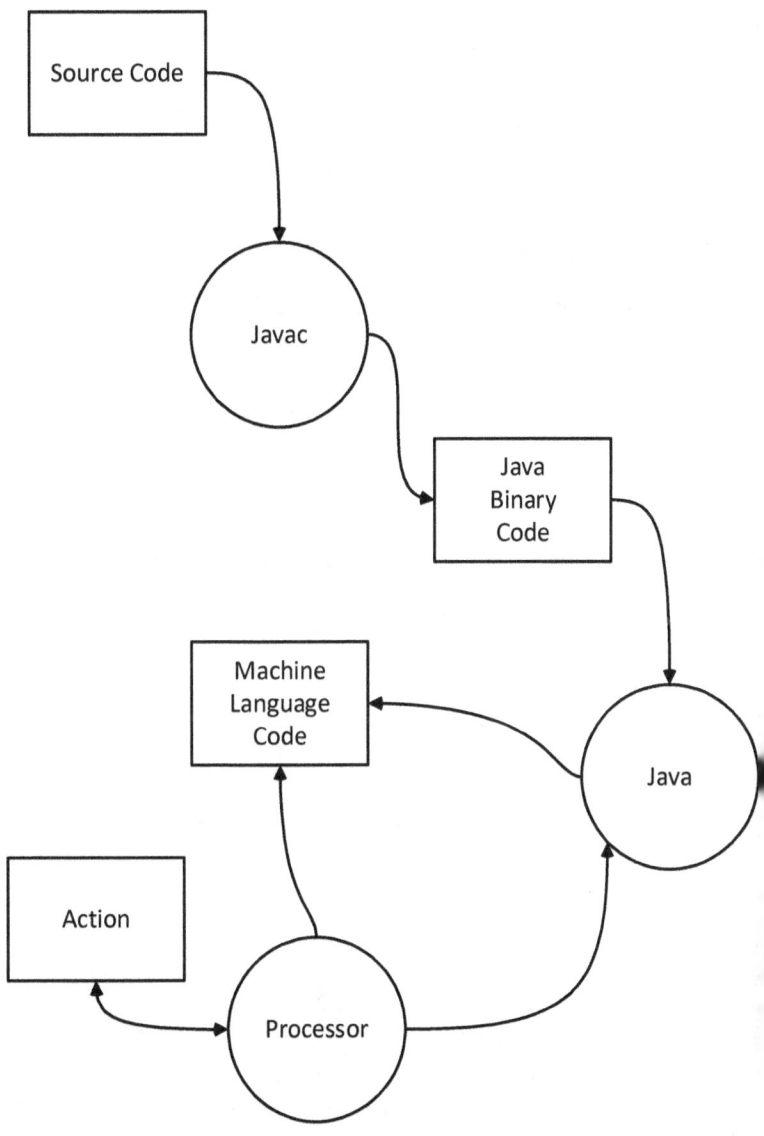

Steps to compile and run a Java program

Assuming that you have loaded the compiler into your machine or are using the class Windows flashdrive, and have setup up the PATH (to reach javac) and CLASSPATH (to reach the directory and import files) system variables correctly, you can run the compiler on your program file: ProgramName.java as

> javac ProgramName.java

The compiler statement either generates errors, or if error free, the file ProgramName.class. If there are no errors, then you can run the program

> java ProgramName

and it will display any output generated or generate run time errors.

Parts of a Compiler

Now let's have a brief discussion on how a Compiler turns your Source code into executable Machine Language, or in the case of javac, into Java Binary Code. This discussion will help you in your future efforts to debug programs. Understanding the parts of the compiler will help you see why:

- One minor error generates many compiler errors.
- Fixing one error seems to generate other errors.

- Compilers will not find all of your logic errors.

The compiler consists of many parts. Each part has a function. And if the errors cause the portion of the compiler to lose track of where it is, it will quit reporting on errors or start generating bogus errors.

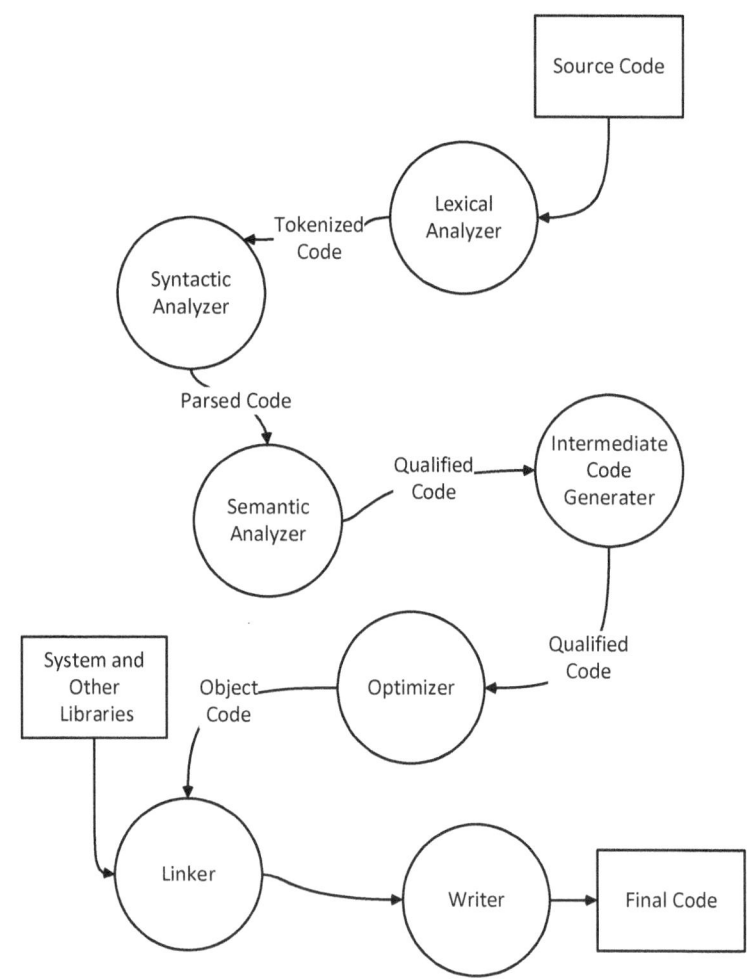

Lexical Analyzer (some discussions call this the Tokenizer; others combine this with the Syntactic Analyzer to call it the Parser).

Basically, the Lexical Analyzer:
- Reads the code.
- Removes comments

- Takes every Variable, Constant, and Method name, etc and converts it into a token.
- Converts numbers to internal form.
- Identifies keywords.

Probable errors are anything that can cause it to lose track of what it is doing. For instance:

- Paired symbols ("", {}, ())
- If you are missing the beginning symbol, then the lexical analyzer will try to scan all of the code as though it wasn't affected by the missing symbol, e.g., a missing double quote would be treated as though it wasn't a string with the expected hilarious results. Note: It usually knows when to expect a brace or parentheses, so it may give you a useful error. With code blocks (braces) it will give you unintelligent error messages.
- If you are missing the ending symbol, the lexical analyzer will keep searching until it finds any matching end symbol, e.g., anything after the beginning double quote will be treated as a string. Of course, everything after the second double quote, will not be, so then see (a). With Code blocks, it may tell you that it runs out of code to parse. With parentheses it may give you an understandable error message.
- A messed-up comment (//, /* */)
- Who knows what it will find in a missing comment symbol?
- In the case of a non-line comment how does it know when the comment ends?
- Some bad syntax on expressions or assignment statements.

- Missing semicolons.

Syntactic Analyzer. The next step would be to make sure to check your statements against the rules of the language, e.g., the Grammar. This step would make sure that: if statements, for loops, etc., make sense. I'm not sure, what exact errors would be generated, but I believe that these would be errors like:

- Having an equivalence (==) instead of equals (=) in an assignment statement.
- Missing semicolons.
- Missing where clauses in do loops.
- Miss-matching if /else groups.
- Incorrect formats for Class or method headers.

Semantic Analyzer. The Lexical and Syntactic Analyzers only verify that the program consists of tokens arranged in a syntactically valid combination. Now we'll move forward to semantic analysis, where we delve even deeper to check whether they form a sensible set of instructions in the programming language. Note: This does not check into whether a reference may be defined elsewhere. Types of errors:

- You do not define a variable correctly, e.g., you changed case on a variable name, or you forgot to define a variable.
- You misused a variable type. You should have used String, when you used int.
- You have code that can never be reached.

Intermediate code generator. This generates as much code as it can without external code libraries. It leaves place holders for external code. There probably aren't too many errors in this step, since theoretically most of the internal code errors have already been found.

Optimizer really depends on the system and language. Some can be quite sophisticated. Some can be very basic. They may go so far as to modify loops to make them more efficient or they may do nothing.

Linker. The linkage process goes out to the external libraries and fills in the place holders. There are several kinds of libraries:
- Language Libraries
- Company Libraries
- Personal libraries
- Operating System Libraries

Errors: The only error is when it cannot find something. In java the error is:
Can't find Symbol - You are probably not importing the library or calling a method incorrectly. Check your capitalization.

Writer then writes out the final Executable File.

Java only differs from a standard compiler in a couple of ways. Since it does not generate an executable, and since it is machine independent, the biggest differences are in the Optimizer, the Linker, and the Writer.

- The Optimizer does essentially nothing. All optimizations are in the system specific libraries.
- The linker links everything except the Operating System Libraries. These are left for the Java Virtual Machine.
- The Writer writes the Java Binary code or the .class files.

The Java Virtual machine (JVM) or java is much more efficient than a normal interpreter since the code is not source code. The code is already parsed, organized, and set up for the interpreter. All structures are set up so that it is not just read in line by line and turned into machine code. I do not pretend to understand the inner processing, but it is quite efficient.

Review

From the compiler standpoint, there are only a few types of languages:

- Machine
- Assembler
- Compiled
- Interpreted
- Hybrid

The parts of a compiler can be described as:

- Lexical Analyzer
- Syntactic Analyzer
- Semantic Analyzer
- Intermediate Code Generator
- Optimizer
- Linker
- Writer

Most of your coding errors are going to crop up in the Lexical, Syntactic, and Semantic Analyzers. The Linker will show errors when it cannot find a reference. With Java, this will most likely occur because you do not have your personal libraries in your CLASSPATH or you have misspelled a method or class or you have forgotten to import a package.

Remember, the compiler can only detect errors in the language. It cannot detect errors in your thinking. These are also referred to as logic errors.

Questions

1. A compiler turns _____ code into _____ code.
2. An Assembler is used to turn Assembly Language into _____ .
3. The Lexical Analyzer turns variable names into _____ .
4. The _____ gets methods from libraries and adds them to your final code.
5. Java is a _____ language
   a) Machine
   b) Compiled
   c) Assembly
   d) Interpreted
   e) Hybrid
6. Most Operating System Command Languages are _____ languages.
   a) Machine
   b) Compiled
   c) Assembly
   d) Interpreted
   e) Hybrid
7. Without humans, computers understand
   a) English
   b) Machine Language
   c) Java
   d) Zero and One
   e) Basic
8. Most coding errors will show up in the
   a) Lexical Analyzer
   b) Syntactic Analyzer
   c) Semantic Analyzer
   d) All of the above
9. The Java compiler command is _____ .

10. The Java Virtual Machine (JVM) is a/an
   _____.

Chapter 3. Java Naming Conventions and Components

Java has several components. You give each component a name when you use it. Unlike some languages the Java rules for naming are almost identical for all components.

Java Components

The components include (but are not limited to):

- Packages - combine class files into groups for security, functionality, and distribution.
- Classes and Objects – top level holders of other components.
- Variables aka attributes. These hold values.
- Methods – these hold code that act.

Naming Rules

The naming rules are:

- Start all names with a letter, dollar sign ($), or underscore (_). I would always use a letter to make code readable.
- All subsequent characters can be any combination of letters, numbers, dollar sign, or underscore.

- All words are case sensitive. OneWord is not the same as oneword. I would not put a lowercase and uppercase version of the same words in a set of code. It is too easy to get them confused.
- You may not use reserved words as your name, such as class, int, extends, etc. See Appendix B for a list of Java reserved words.
- You should (must) follow your organizations rules.
- Make names meaningful.

I like to use nouns to name Variables, Classes, and Objects and verbs to name Methods.

There are two prevailing naming conventions in most languages:

One called CamelCase, uses mashed words with the subsequent words capitalized. Sometimes the first word is capitalized usually not. This looks like:

    gearBox
    GearBox
    ChangeGears

The other called snake case, uses lower case letters and underscores to separate the letters.

    gear_box
    change_gears

Since snake case is mostly a holdover from c, and CamelCase is mostly used in Java, I will use CamelCase.

Note: constants are usually all capitals, e.g., GRAVITY

Symbols

Your most common symbol is the semicolon ";". Every java statement must end with a semicolon. This is extremely important and ends up being the most common error. Another common error is adding a semicolon before you want one and ending up with a null or incomplete statement.

The basic paired code Symbols used in Java are parentheses (), braces {}, brackets [], and greater than/less than symbols<>. This is a brief definition of each, we will go into more definition later as we use them.

Parentheses () are used in several ways, besides in their normal math and logical methods, they are used to denote logical expressions and methods. For methods they are used to hold parameter lists.

Braces {} are used at the beginning and end of all code blocks. Including, but not limited to class templates, methods, if statements, and loops. I recommend placing a comment on the end brace tying the brace to the beginning brace. When we start debugging code, it is easy to lose track of which brace belongs to which and the compiler can quickly lose track when you are missing a brace.

44

Brackets [] are used for arrays.

Greater than/Less than Symbols <> are used to allow the compiler to know which types to limit certain classes to use. For instance, if the term <String> is used for a ArrrayList definition then the compiler will only allow types String to fill the ArrayList. These are only used by the compiler.

Comments.

There are two sets of symbols used for comments.

// is used for line comments. Anything on the line following the // is a comment. Anything on that line before the // is not a comment. These can be on their own line or at the end of a line of code. Personally, I prefer to use them on their own line.

```
// is a line comment
```

The paired symbols /* and */ are a block comment that can encompass multiple lines. This is very useful for temporarily commenting out code. Notice that I said temporarily. In other words:

```
/*


        is a comment block


*/
```

As we discovered in our discussion of the compiler comments are tossed out during the parse phase of the compilation. So you can use as many comments as you please. It will not affect the efficiency of your code, it may affect the ability to understand your code.

Java Components

Packages

We will not be building packages in this class. Java provides a number of packages in their libraries with useful statements. We will introduce them as we need them.

There is one package that is added automatically and does not need to be imported. This package is java.lang. For instance, String and System.out are two of the classes in java.lang.

However, in order for the Linker to find most of the packages, you need to include the import statement before the class statement in your code. For instance, if you wanted to use any class from the util package you would need to:

```
import java.util.*;
```

Notice that I use the * to enable the compiler to include any class from the util package. While you can specify specific classes from util, there is no

46

benefit to be gained from specifying a specific one. The Linker will only include the ones it needs. It is not more efficient to specify the classes that you need. Therefore my recommendation is to always use the ".*".

I have included a package called CSCI for this set of courses to use. To use these classes, you need to:

```
import CSCI.*;
```

If you get the "Can't find Symbol" error and it pertains to a method from a package probably means that you either:

Did not import the proper package.
Misspelled the method (look at case).
Have the wrong types on the argument list.
In the case of CSCI, you do not have the directory in the proper place, e.g., as a subdirectory under the directory where you are compiling your code.

See Appendix C for more information on package CSCI.

So how can you find out what packages you need? I like to use the internet. Another way to check classes is to use the javap command

```
javap java.lang.String
```

which will give you all of the headers on all of the variables and methods of the class String.

Unfortunately, if you have the wrong package name, you will get an error, so if you do not know the package, the internet works better.

One last hint about packages. The format java.util refers to a directory structure. The dot takes place of a directory symbol, so this would be java/util in one of your CLASSPATH directories or one of the standard java directories.

Class

Everything other than the primitive types in Java is a Class or an Object. A class is a template. The class holds variables aka attributes and methods, including the main method. The object is an instantiation of the class. To instantiate a class is to bring it to life. You set aside memory and allow it to be used.

Classes consist of:

        Header
        Constructor
            Method to initialize Object
            Same name as Class
            Does not have a return value
            May or may not have attributes
        Variables
        Methods

Example

```
public class DisplayName{

}
```

This program must be stored in a file by the name DisplayName.java we will get into more details as we go.

Other Classes can be of two types, either static or non-static.

A non-static class must be stored in a file with the same name as the class.

Static Classes, aka inner classes, are contained in classes.

When do you need to instantiate a class?

You should never instantiate your program or main class.
If a class has non-static variables or methods, it must be instantiated.

How do you instantiate a class? By using the keyword new. For instance, the CSCI class FileIn has non-static methods to read data from a File. It has two Constructors, one of which expects the Filename that it will read. Assuming that FileName is a String variable holding the filename, to instantiate a FileIn object Input, the code looks like:

```
FileIn input = new FileIn(filename);
```

FileIn does not have any available variables. (This is called information hiding). It does have two methods. To read a line of data all you need to do is:

```
String dataLine;
dataLine = input.Read();
```

Then when finished

```
input.close();
```

If you have Static Variables or Methods, then you simply use them, without instantiating the object by addressing the class. If you wanted to convert a string to an Integer you could use
CSCIConvert.Parse()
without instantiating the class. (assuming ERROR is an int constant)

```
myInt = CSCIConvert.Parse(dataLine,ERROR);
```

Method

The main method is the initial starting point for a program. Every program must have one and exactly one main method.

The main methods format is mandated by the java interpreter. If you don't have it exactly as written, it won't recognize it.

```
public static void main(String[] args){
}
```

In fact the only thing that you can change is the term args. The variable args[] is a short for arguments and is the string array of command line arguments that you submit when you call the program.
The name args can be changed but is traditional.

The rest of the code for your main method goes between the braces.

If methods belong to our current class, then we run them by stating the name and any parameters or variables that they need like:

```
MethodName(VariableName);
```

If they belong a different class, then we use the dot notation like:

```
System.out.Println(AnyString);
```

So, before we write any additional code, our first program looks like:

```
public class DisplayName{
  public static void main(String[] args){
  }
}
```

This will compile but will do nothing.

So, let us add some simple code to it and compile and run it.

```
// class header
public class DisplayName{
// main program header must be copied exactly
public static void main(String[] args ) {
        // static method to print out to standard out.
        // Glen K. Blood is a string
        // "" are used to enclose a string
        System.out.println("Glen K. Blood");
} //end main
}//end GBloodDisplayName
```

System.out.println() is a library method to print a String variable to the screen. It automatically adds a return at the end. You will use this method all the time.

"Glen K. Blood" is a hardcoded String. The double quotes ("") are used to enclose a String. You can change this to be your name.

Save this to our compilation directory as DisplayName.java

The name of the class must match the file name, including capitalization.

After you have set up the compiler, according to Appendix A (You will have to do this exercise every time you enter the command window.):

Type: **javac DisplayName.java** to build the java binary file

Type: **java DisplayName** to run the program

Glen K. Blood is displayed.

52

And you have run your first program.

We will get more into methods in a later chapter.

Variables

These are also known as attributes. These describe the class or object. You can think of them as nouns or adjectives. Variables have the following characteristics:

- They have a name.
- They have a Data Type (to be discussed in a later chapter).
- They have a memory Location.
- They can be changed in your program at runtime.

There are some basic types of class variables

Static variables – have a single copy of the variables for all objects instantiated from that class. You can think of these as Global variables. I would never use these for reasons that we will see later.

Non-static variables – These are not allowed in your program class. These are used in your class as variables. You will see how to define them in the Data Types Chapter. These are very useful in Stamp Data and methods.

Constants – These use the keyword final. Usually the keywords final and static are used together. The only difference between constants and variables is that the value can only change when you modify and recompile the code. You cannot change constants at runtime. This is the only time that I would recommend (or condone) the regular use of static variables in your program. Constants are usually designated by using all capitals.

Writing Clean Readable Code

The basic Rules for writing clean readable code are very simple:

Comment well

Provide Headers to every class that explains what the class does. Explain the inputs and outputs. If there are tricks to the algorithms, explain the algorithms. If there are source books for the algorithms, you might cite your sources.

In your code explain your logic. Especially where the code is not self- documenting.

Avoid over commenting to the point where comments may be cumbersome to be maintained.

Avoid commenting out old unused code. Some companies encourage it as a practice to maintain versioning. Eventually, the commented-out code is longer than the real code. Personally, I feel that it makes code very hard to read. If keeping old code is important, use versioning software to maintain old copies of the code. Or keep it long enough for some testing and then clean it up.

Standards

Use good naming conventions for all Objects, Variables, and Methods.

Use spacing and indentation.
Avoid programming tricks that produce really tight code unless you need them for performance. You (or your replacement) may not recognize them when revision is required. Remember, you always face time constraints and pressure when working. I think of code written this way as write-once code. I have avoided mentioning such tricks in this text.

Be consistent. If you develop a set of techniques in your coding style, unless there is a good reason to change them, stick with them. There are several good reasons for this practice. Chances are you will make fewer mistakes, you can develop your personal library, code and tests, and your speed will increase. However, do not be afraid to learn something new.

There are more standards outlined in Appendix D.

Review

There are four basic components in Java

- Packages - combine class files into groups for security, functionality, and distribution.
- Classes and Objects – top level holders of other components.
- Variables aka attributes. These hold values
- Methods – these hold code that do things.

Java has a consistent set of rules for naming components. They basically boil down to:

- Start all names with a letter, dollar sign ($), or underscore (_). I would always use a letter.
- All subsequent characters can be any combination of letters, numbers, dollar sign, or underscore.
- All words are case sensitive. OneWord is not the same as oneword.
- You may not use reserved words as your name, such as class, int, extends, etc.
- You should follow your organizations rules.
- Make names meaningful.

There are some symbols recognized by the compiler. Some are paired symbols

"{}" – used for code blocks

"[]" – Used for arrays

"◇" used for type casting in collections.

"()" used for expressions, and method parameter lists

Some are specialized symbols such as mathematical symbols, * - / and logical symbols, && || !.

The comment Symbols "//" "/* */" are special.

Remember that the backslash "\" in a char or string is an escape character and has to be handled specially.

Variables have four characteristics

1. They have a name.
2. They have a Data Type.
3. They have a memory Location.
4. They can be changed in your program at runtime.

Constants (keyword final) have every characteristic that variables do except for #4, they cannot be changed.

We also gave some rules for writing good clean readable code. These included:

- Comments
- Spaces and indentation
- Using good conventions and standards
- Avoiding tricks.
- Being Consistent.

Questions

1. Objects are_____classes
   a) Instantiated from
   b) Unrelated to
   c) Inherited from
   d) Used to define
2. Java Classes are not composed of:
   a) Headers
   b) Packages
   c) Constructors
   d) Variables
   e) Methods
3. Component Names may start with
   a) A letter or certain symbols
   b) Any alphanumeric
   c) Any number.
4. It is recommended that you use the following rules for naming except:
   a) Use meaningful names
   b) Follow your organizational rules.
   c) Limit yourself to six characters to make the names easy to type.
   d) Avoid Java reserve words.
   e) Maintain consistent capitalization.
5. Java Components include everything except:
   a) Variables
   b) Classes
   c) Objects
   d) Programs
   e) Methods
   f) Packages
6. Constants lack one feature of non-constant variables. Which one?
   a) They have a name
   b) They have a Data Type

c) They have a memory Location.

d) They can be changed in your program at runtime.

7. Which keyword is used to tell the linker to find a package?

a) find

b) import

c) package

d) goto

8. If you want to use the static method eat, for the class George. eat returns nothing. There are no parameters in eat. Which is the proper syntax?

a) George.eat();

b) George.execute(eat)

c) eat()

d) George myGeorge = new George(); myGeorge.eat();

9. Which method must appear in every program and denotes the starting point of the program?

a) start();

b) main();

c) program();

d) init();

10. When you use the keyword static in front of a variable in your class:

a) One memory location is created, and every object created from it shares that variable.

b) It is a constant shared by every object created from it.

c) It is a class variable and every object created from it has access to its own copy of it.

Chapter 4. Data Types

Bits and Bytes

The computer processor and memory works in
binary, or zero and one. These are referred to as
bits.

```
Bit
0 or 1
```

These bits are usually grouped in sets of eight bits
or a byte.

Byte							
0	1	2	3	4	5	6	7

Most computers work in some number of bytes.
Bytes can hold unsigned integers from 0 to 127.
The oldest microcomputer processors used 1 byte
or 8 bits, later they graduated to 2 Bytes or 16 bits.
Most computer processors and operating systems
today can handle at least 32 or 64 bits. Windows
comes in either of these two flavors. 64-bit

Windows will support most programs built for the 32-bit Platform.

Every memory location in a computer has an address. This is usually denoted as a Hexadecimal (base 16) number with a range based on the number of bits that the operating System has.

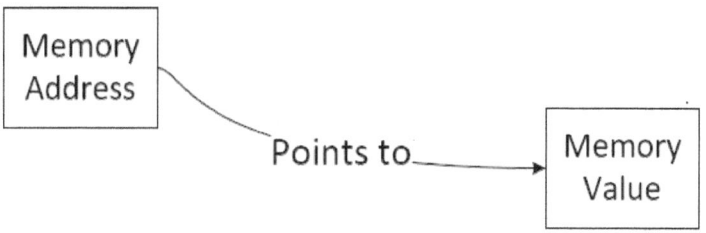

For instance, theoretically, a 32-bit Windows System can access 2^{32} addresses or 4 billion addresses (4 GB addresses). If each memory location held 32 bits, then this system could theoretically hold 128 GB of memory. Since a 64-bit processor could theoretically hold 2^{64} addresses at 64 bits per address = 1.5×10^{56} GB of memory. Of course, this is only theoretical, they don't really access that much memory and besides you couldn't afford it.

Larger processors do allow you to access larger numbers for mathematical operations, which on an 8-bit computer was a real issue.

Even given the binary system, computers by themselves could only understand unsigned integers.

Mathematicians, Computer Scientists, and Language developers have developed a system of codes that map the unsigned integers to different data types. This allows these memory locations to be used as data. These are known as the basic data types. These basic data types are usually grouped into numeric, String, and Boolean. In Java code, these are called the Primitive data types.

Primitive Data Types

Primitive Variables

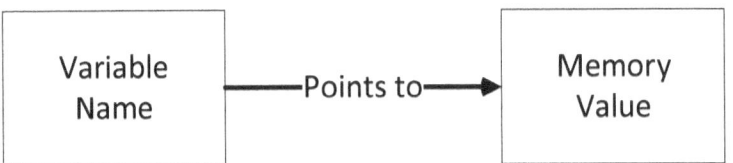

The variable name of a Primitive data type is its memory location and denotes the actual value. For instance, one of the basic types, is int (or 32 bit signed integer). To define a primitive type you give its type and name, for instance:

```
int Counter;
```

You can define more the one variable, as long as they are of the same type (I believe this can be less readable):

```
int Counter, Distance, GeoStationaryAngle;
```

Alternatively, you can set an initial value for the variable:

```
int Counter = 0;
```

The primitive data types are always passed by value. This means that when they are passed into a method, the value is copied into a new memory location.

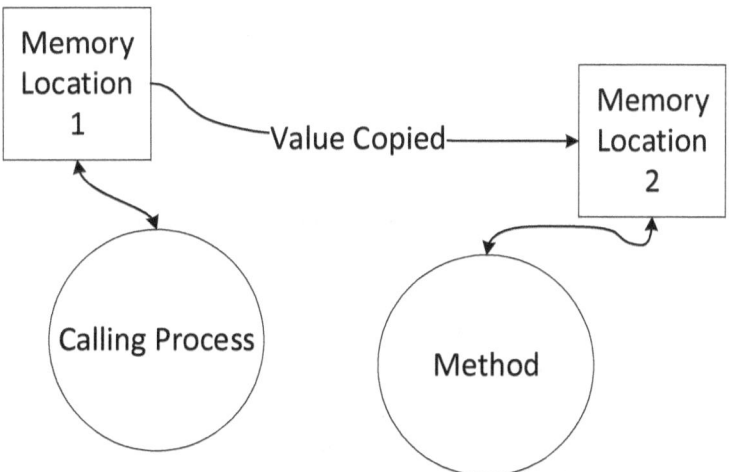

This second memory location is then used by the method. Any changes do not affect the calling routines variable. Therefore, when you return from the method, your original value is unchanged. We will discuss this in more detail later.

Java numeric values have two types signed integer (-x to x) and floating point. There are no unsigned integers in the primitive types.

Signed integers

Signed Integers only differ in the number of bits they use, which controls the range that they allow. If x represents the number of bits they use, then the formula for the range is: -2^{x-1} to $2^{x-1}-1$. The integer types are:

Bits	Name	Range
8	byte	-2^7 to 2^7-1
16	short	-2^{15} to $2^{15}-1$
32	int	-2^{31} to $2^{31}-1$
64	long	-2^{63} to $2^{63}-1$

I would use int most of the time. Most computers today are at least 32 bits and int gives you a large range of data. The Java Math libraries expect type int, and most of the time, your space requirements will not be tight enough to require you to use the smaller types.

I do want to caution you about integer division. Java integer division only occurs when all elements in a division equation are integers. This is true of most programming languages. In this case the remainder or fractional portion is lost. It is not rounded, it is lost. So, $99/100 = 0$. There are programmatic uses for this, but only a few.

Floating Point Numbers

There are no real numbers in the computer. There are only floating-point representations. These are 32 and 64-bit IEEE 754 standard floating-point notation. You can think of them as scientific notation, but in binary. These numbers are not precise, and you cannot directly control the number of decimals in our calculations.

How are they represented?

The numbers are separated into a sign bit(s), a Mantissa (m) and an exponent e (e). For informational purposes, the formula for float is:

$$(-1)^s x \, m \, x \, 2^{e-127}$$

The allows float to use 1 bit for the sign, 8 bits for the exponent, and 23 bits for the mantissa and gives you about 6 to 7 decimal point precision.

The formula for double is similar except that there are more bits available for the mantissa and exponent.

Which one should we use normally? I would suggest float, except that all of the Math library classes expect double. So I would recommend sticking to double, since you will need the math libraries at some point.

```
double PI = 3.14159;
double Radius;
```

String Data

Character Data (char). The basic type of String Data is Character. Characters are a single Alphanumeric, (A, B, C, ..., 1, 2, 3...) and a number of non-character symbols (#, @, !, %...). Most computers use one of two codes for Character data. ASCII (**American Standard Code for Information Interchange)** or Unicode. Java uses Unicode which is a superset of ASCII. ASCII uses one byte to represent each number or character. Unicode uses two. While ASCII is pretty much limited to the English characters and some symbols, Unicode also gives you most of the international characters. To give you a rough idea of the encoding scheme:

Byte Value	Characters
48-57	0-9
65-90	A-Z
97-122	a-z

Unicode uses the same codes for these characters.

Here are some interesting facts about the letter code values:

The capital letters are exactly 32 less than their lower case equivalents.

They are numerically in order but case dependent ('a' < 'b', but 'a' > 'B').

Therefore, comparing mixed case character strings is not a trivial problem.

char

```
char   mychar;
char Sex = 'M';
```

Character constants are denoted by a pair of single quotes 'a'.

As a single variable, char is not generally useful, unless you are playing with individual parts of Strings.

Strings

Strings in any language are a collection of characters. There are several ways that these are implemented. Some languages, such as FORTRAN, do not define a separate String data Type.

There are three basic ways that languages define Strings.

- As a character array with a pre-defined end character such as linefeed. Strings defined this way are usually limited to one line of data at a time. The only issue with this method is that you must use a special method to include this character within your array.
- As a Character Array with Fixed Length. You define the length in your code. The extra data is then filled with blanks.
- As a Character Array and a separate Integer length variable.

Java chose the third method. Java implements the String datatype as a class, but often treats it as a primitive value. While String is not exactly a Primitive variable, it is passed by Value. There are several ways to define a String.

```
String myString;
String myString = new String();
String myString = "Fred";
```

Strings are not stored like normal variables. Each String variable is not stored in its own location in memory. There is a String pool in memory. Each unique String is stored there. So if you have two String variables:

```
String Alpha = "Fred";
String Beta = "Fred";
```

Alpha and Beta's Strings do not point to different memory locations. There is only one memory location (in a String common pool) that has "Fred" as a String. That memory location does not change. If you change Alpha or Beta a new memory location is created and a new string is built. Then the variable is pointed to it. I have not been able to find out what happens when neither Alpha nor Beta point to "Fred", I assume that it is removed from the String Pool. For this reason, it is recommended that String is not used for variant Strings, but this is beyond the scope of this course.

One other limitation of Strings is that if you attempt to load a set of data into a String variable and that data has a linefeed embedded in it '\n', the string will stop loading at the linefeed. So, if you plan to build a set of paragraphs, plan to use multiple Strings.

Since String is a Reference type it has several built-in methods. Some of these are:

```
int length();
boolean isEmpty();
void getChars(char[], int);
boolean equals(Object);
boolean equalsIgnoreCase(String);
int compareTo(String);
int compareToIgnoreCase(String);
public static java.lang.String
format(java.lang.String,
java.lang.Object...);
int indexOf(String);
int indexOf(String, int);
String substring(int);
String concat(String);
String replace(char, char);
boolean matches(String);
boolean contains(CharSequence);
String replace(CharSequence,
CharSequence);
String[] split(String);
String toLowerCase();
String toUpperCase();
String trim();
```

We will discuss how to use several of them in as we need them.

One fun method is the format method. This is a simple way to build a clean output. The method is based on the c languages' formatting scheme. The first argument is a format command. Subsequent arguments are the variables used in your formatted string. The way I like to do this is to build a formatted string and then use that string. Suppose you have a name and age and you want to format it into nice columns. You might set it up as:

```
String format = "%20s  %3d";
String line = String.format(format,name,age);
```

What do the format codes mean. You can put anything into the format String. It will duplicate the string. If you precede it with a percent sign, "%", this means that it is a format code. The number is the minimum number of spaces that it will use (if you need more Java will use more, so be careful). The "s" means that it expects a String and the "d" means that it expects an integer. If you use an "f" it will expect a floating point. With floating points you can use a decimal point after the number to say how many decimal places to display. The period and the numbers after the period will count in the total number of places. A minus sign after the "%", "%-" means to left justify the output. A subset of the codes are as follows:

```
's', 'S'        String
'c', 'C'        character
'd'             integer
'f'             floating point
't', 'T'        date/time
'%'             literal '%'
'n'             line separator
```

Boolean

Boolean data has two possible values (True, False) and is used in decision making. This is one of my favorite data types. If a language, such as FORTRAN or c, does not have one, I always built Boolean constants, just to make code readable. Well, Java has a Boolean data type, called boolean.

boolean data type. The boolean type only has two possible values true, or false (lower case). I have been unable to find out any documentation on the storage size, so I assume that this is implementation/machine dependent.

```
boolean isTrue;
boolean ifthen = true;
boolean maybe = false;
```

Reference Data Types

Reference Variables

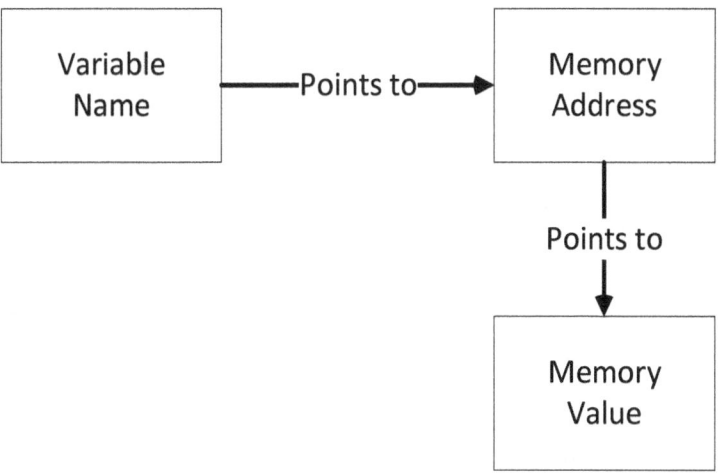

All other Data types are in Java are Reference Data Types. This means that they point to the memory location of the data, not to the Value. This has a few repercussions.

When you pass them into a Method, you are passing by reference. This means that you pass the address of the data, not the value.

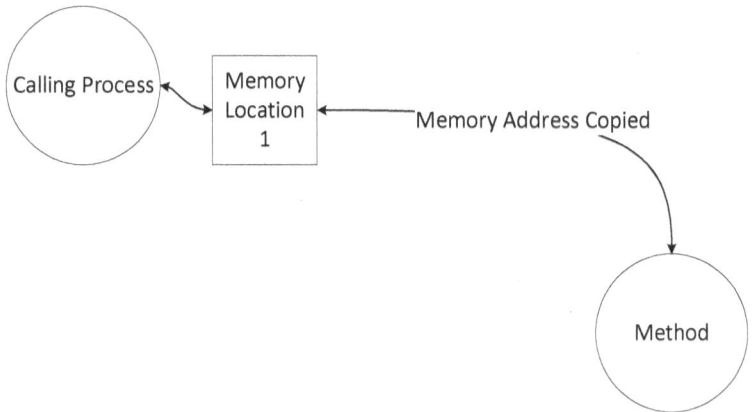

Therefore, if you change the value of the variable within the routine, you will change the value of the variable when you return from the routine. If you do this without expecting it, this is called a side effect.

Your variable name is also known as a pointer. This means that when you use the assignment statement A = B or equivalence statement (A == B), you are exchanging and comparing addresses and not the Value. Be careful and use the appropriate method.

Stamp Data

It is often useful to combine the primitive or reference data types into a single package. This is referred to as Stamp Data or User Defined Data Types (UDT) For instance, if you have an input or output data file, it is very useful to define a data type that holds all of the data in the record of that file. Let's say that we had a comma separated value (.csv) file with Name, height, and weight. That first few records might look like:

Kaden Diaz,65,242
Indigo Chaney,65,183
Harlan Hooper,71,200
Kato Mckinney,62,233
Rinah Norton,63,164
Eleanor Padilla,73,201
Quamar Ramos,66,177

While you could define three different variables:

```
String Name;
int Height;
int Weight;
```

Every time you wanted to pass this person, you would have to keep track of each of the three variables and make sure that they were in synch. Hence the usefulness of a UDT.

You can think of a Class as a Type Definition, or Template. An Object is the variable or **instantiation**. Objects are always passed by reference. For this course, we will define classes in our main class. These are referred to as inner or static classes. Therefore, inner Classes are defined in the following way:

```
public static class Record{
        public String Name;
        public int Height;
        public int Weight;
} // end class Record
```

Defined within the class, but outside of the main, just like a method. Like class variables, I like to put inner classes at the beginning of the class structure.

You then define the objects like:

```
Record Person1 = new Record();
Record Person2 = new Record();
```

And you use them using the dot (.) notation.

```
// Load First Person
Person1.Name = " Kaden Diaz ";
Person1.Height = 65;
Person1.Weight = 242;

// Load Second Person
Person2.Name = " Kaden Diaz ";
Person2.Height = 65;
Person2.Weight = 183;

// Print out results

System.out.println(Person1.Name + " "
+ Person1.Height + " " + Person1.Weight);
System.out.println(Person2.Name + " "
+ Person2.Height + " " + Person2.Weight);
```

And your output is:

Kaden Diaz 65 242
Indigo Chaney 65 183

As you can see this can be very powerful.

System Types

There are so many system types that it is impossible to list. Like the UDTs, these are all classes. They include variables and methods. As we go through this course, I will introduce you to the ones that we will use. If you want to use more, you can ask or use the internet to research them. There are a couple of things you need to understand in order to use them.

Classes come in two types utility and non-utility.

Utility classes hold a set of static methods (and constants) and do not need to be instantiated. In other words, you do not need to build an object to hold them. You use the method by stating the class name dot and method name. Example math.abs(mydouble) returns the absolute value of the double mydouble.

Non-utility classes have to be instantiated into an object to be used. So, to build a Date object you would specify:

```
Date current_time = new Date();
```

Location. Each class belongs to a package. A package provides a secure, convenient place to maintain the class. Many of the classes that we use belong to Java.lang, e.g., Math, which is automatically imported. Other system classes belong to a package that must be manually imported into our code: For example. Java.util holds ArrayList and Date. So to use either class you would need:

```
import java.util.*;
```

At the start of your program file. While you can specify, import java.util.Date;, there is no advantage and you might be missing something else you need.

Course Defined Data Types

While teaching these courses, I have built a series of static and non-static utilities in a package called CSCI which has been kept on the flashdrive. See Appendix A on the use of the flashdrive. You will need to place:

```
import CSCI.*;
```

With the other imports. And the CSCI folder will have to be in your CLASSPATH. Right now there are methods for getting a formatted current time, reading and writing a Unicode string from/to a data file, checking for an integer or a double, changing a String to an integer or a double and other activities as needed.

Variable Security

You may see the words private or public proceed a variable name. This is to define who can access that variable. Usually in class definitions variables are private and methods are public for information hiding.

Static Variables

The keyword static makes a single copy of that variable for all objects created when you instantiate that class. This variable is a global variable for all objects of that class. If in the main class, this makes it global for the entire program. This means that it can be changed anywhere at any time. This is bad news.

Except when you add the keyword final. Then this becomes a constant, as in:

```
final static int ERROR = 0;
```

Since the value of ERROR cannot be changed at runtime, this is useful and does not suffer from the risks of causing untraceable errors.

Arrays

Arrays are ordered groups of primitive and reference variables. Arrays are passed by reference. Arrays are denoted by the bracket pair []. Arrays are declared in two steps:

Step 1 declares the type:

```
Type[] name;
```

Examples:

```
int[] Ages;
double[] Weights;
string[]   Names;
```

The second step sets the maximum size of the array. This must be defined at compile time. The size can be defined by any integer constant, variable (within a method), or hardcoded integer.

```
Name = new Type[int];
```

Examples

```
final static int AGESIZE = 10;
Ages = new int[10];
Weights = new double[AGESIZE];
Names =   new String[10];
```

Note in java: Arrays are base 0. You start counting from Ages[0], not Ages[1]. You end at Ages[9], not Ages[10].

You will get an ArrayIndexOutofRange runtime error if you address the Ages array at any point beyond 9.

Like the primitive variables, small arrays have an easy way to initialize them (I would not use this method on large arrays). By setting values within braces, you both set initial values to each element of the array and declare the size of the array. For instance:

```
String[] Letters = {"A","B","C","D","E","F"};
```

Defines an array named Letters of size 6 with the first 6 letters of the alphabet.

Array Limitations

You cannot just add or remove elements to/from the middle of the array. You literally must move the other elements to make empty space. This makes sorting expensive in either time or space, sometimes requiring a second copy of the array.

You cannot add space to an array during run time. Therefore, if you size an array for 100 elements and you have 101 elements, you will have a run time error. Therefore, you need to size your arrays for more growth than you expect to need and keep track of your data growth.

While you can have multiple dimension arrays, each array element must have the same data type. Therefore, if you have more than one data type, you must go through additional work which we will discuss in a later chapter.

Using Arrays

Using arrays is very straightforward.

Setting values in arrays

Usually, although this is not required, you start loading an array at zero and continue sequentially. While arrays start at zero, you can address them from any place within their range and in any order. Since the array variable length denotes the maximum size of the array and not how many elements have been filled, it is generally a good idea to build a second variable to keep track of the currently used size of the array. Loading an array:

Single Elements

```
Ages[2] = 34;
Weights[i] = 145;
Names[0] = "George";
```

Getting Values

Just like loading an array element, you use an integer value to get a value. You do have one additional condition, not only do you need to ensure that it is between 0 and the maximum size - 1, you need to make sure that it is in the range of the data that you have filled. While, the system will not give you an error, you may end up with bogus results.

Say you have an array, alpha, with a maximum size of 10, and you have filled the first 5 elements (0 through 4). If you access alpha[7], the system will not give you an error, but you will not get a valid value. However, if you try to access alpha[12], you will get an error.

Assignment Statements

```
A = Ages[4];
B = Weights[i];
myName = Names[8];
```

Using Arrays in Methods

Method declaration: Use the same form as the array declaration:

```
public static returntype MethodName(type[] arrayname){}
public static double CalcAverage(int[] Numbers){}
```

Since you defined the array in the method header, you can use the array without redefining it inside the method. You do need to be careful that you do not attempt to address any elements that are beyond the maximum size of the array.

Method call: Just use the array name:

```
Response = MethodName(arrayname);
Answer = CalcAverage(Numbers);
```

Note: Arrays are a reference type so any changes to array values are reflected upon return from the method.

You can also define the Array as a return type. This actually allows you to build the array size within the routine. For instance, there is a method in FileIn that allows you to read a file into a String array

```
public String[] readArray()
```

You would then call it like:

```
String[] records;
FileIn myFile = new FileIn(filename);
records = readArray();
```

The length parameter would give you the size of the array.

```
int size = records.length;
```

Array Methods

Arrays have built in methods. You can find all of them by typing javap java.lang.Arrays in a windows command line.

Two of the useful commands are sort() and binarySearch.

We had the array names we read in from the last section.

To sort the Array, you would simply use the command:

```
Arrays.sort(names);
```

Once you have sorted names, you could use the binarySearch command to find the position of any name you wanted:

```
Position = Arrays.binarySearch(names,anyName);
```

Do not attempt this method unless the names array has been sorted. Binary search algorithms will not work unless the input data has been sorted.

A final data type is ArrayList.

ArrayList

ArrayList has three major benefits over arrays:

1. You do not define a maximum size at compile time. ArrayList grows as you expand it.
2. You can add to or delete from the middle of ArrayList without penalty.
3. Arraylist has a built in method called size() to tell you the current used size of the ArrayList.

The biggest difference in ArrayList is that instead of directly using braces to address the individual members, e.g., [i], you have to use methods, such as:

- add(e) adds an element to end of the ArrayList.
- get(int) gets the element from the position on the Arraylist as specified on the index.
- set(int,e)   sets the element from the position on the Arraylist as specified on the index.

One hint. When you add a reference type to an Arraylist. Make sure that you create a new element. Otherwise you may end up with an ArrayList with n copies of the same memory location.

The first step in using an ArrayList is to make sure that you import the correct java library.

```
import java.util.*;
```

Defining an ArrayList is a little different than an array. You don't actually set aside space for the ArrayList or define the type of the ArrayList. You do give the compiler a hint of what type to expect using <type>.

```
ArrayList <recordType> record =
          new ArrayList<recordType>();
```

Note this <Reference Type> is a compiler hint. It is not a runtime instruction. Hence, it is not included in the method signature. Therefore, you cannot have two methods with the same name and the same parameters except for Arraylists with different <Reference Type>;

```
Build(ArrayList<Person>  People);
Build(Arraylist<Dog> Dogs);
```

These two methods are not allowed. Even though Person and Dog are different Reference types

Using ArrayLists

Using arraylists is very straightforward.

Let us define a reference type and an ArrayList.

```
public static record{
        String name;
        int     age;
}

record person;

ArrayList<record> people = new ArrayList<record>();
```

Setting values in arraylists:

There are two methods. To add an element to the end of the ArrayList, use add

Single Elements:

```
person = new record();
person.name = "George"
person.age = 24;
people.add(person);
person = new record();
person.name = "Amy"
person.age = 32;
people.add(person);
```

We have just added two different people, George and Amy. They will appear as sequential records. Notice that we created a new object in between each add. If we had not done that Amy's information would have overridden George's and both entries would have pointed to the same record, Amy's. George would no longer exist.

Let's say, that we wanted to insert someone in between George and Amy. This is quite easy. We know that George is at position 0, since he was added first and Amy is at position 1, since she was added immediately after, so we will add Bill in position 1, using the set method.

```
person = new record();
person.name = "Bill"
person.age = 45;
people.set(1,person);
```

So, where did Amy end up. Amy is now in position 2. When a record is inserted in the middle of an ArrayList, all subsequent records are automatically bumped up one position at little or no cost. This is a great advantage over arrays. One risk of using the set method. You can end up with gaps in your data. You can also have errors if you try to set data where you have not allocated space.

You can get the actual size of the ArrayList by using the method size().

```
int size = people.size();
```

Getting Values

Just like getting an array element, you use an integer value to get a value from an ArrayList, using the method get(int);

Assignment Statements

```
String name;
int age;
record person;

person = People.get(2);

name = person.name;
age = person.age;
```

Using ArrayLists in Methods

Method declaration: Use the same form as the array declaration:

```
public static returntype MethodName(ArrayList<type> list){}
public static double CalcAverageAge(ArrayList<record> people){}
```

Since you defined the ArrayList in the method header, you can use the array without redefining it inside the method.

Method call: Just use the ArrayList name:

```
Response = MethodName(list);
Answer = CalcAverageAge(people);
```

Note: ArrayLists are a reference type so any changes to ArrayList values are reflected upon return from the method.

You can also define the Array as a return type. This actually allows you to build the array size within the routine. For instance, there is a method in FileIn that allows you to read a file into a String ArrayList

```
public ArrayList<String> readList()
```

You would then call it like:

```
ArrayList<String> records;
FileIn myFile = new FileIn(filename);
records = readList();
```

You would then process the records of the file.

You can get the actual size of the ArrayList by using the method size().

```
int size = records.size();
```

Review

There are two basic types of data in Java, primitive and reference. Primitive types point to the actual value. Reference types point to the memory location that holds the data. Primitive types are all predefined data types that are divided into Integer, Floating Point, Char, and Boolean. Integer and floating point are further divided into several types based on the number of bytes that hold the data. I recommend that you normally use:

- int
- double
- boolean
- String (not exactly a Primitive data type),

Reference data types are the bulk of the data types. In Java they are all classes. Reference data types all pass by reference (hence the name) into methods. So, if you change the value in the method, you change the value in the calling variable.

You can define your own reference data types. You can also use the built in System libraries. The system library classes include variables and methods.

Arrays, while useful are limited in that the

- Maximum size must be defined at compile Time.
- Moving data in the array is expensive.

Arrays are
- Base zero.
- Can be addressed anywhere within range.
- Passed by reference

ArrayLists

- Are limited to reference data.
- Must use the get, add, set methods.
- Maximum size is not defined.
- Moving or adding data is cheap

Questions

1. We will be using the following recommended java datatypes in this course
   a) Alphanumeric, real, and Boolean
   b) String, int, double, and boolean
   c) Char, byte, float, and Long
   d) Numeric, String, and Boolean
   e) None of the above
2. The two normal ways that computers use to encode characters are _____ and _____.
3. Java primitive types are passed by _____.
4. Most of java types are reference types. This means that when you pass them into a method and change them without meaning to you can cause a

   _____ _____.
5. String variables are the only reference type that is passed by _____.
6. Which of the following is not a valid integer type definition:
   a) int Apple;
   b) int Apple = 1;
   c) int Apple, Orange;
   d) int Apple = 'a';
   e) int Apple = INTCONSTANT; //
      INCONSTANT is an int constant.
7. Which answer is incorrect about boolean data types?
   a) They help clarify code;
   b) The small size of the data type is efficient.
   c) They are a simple way to set an intermediate boolean expression value.
   d) They complete the data type set.
8. Stamp data is useful to:
   a) Group related data together
   b) Group random stuff together for convenience.

    c) Not useful at all.
9. Computer Real Numbers are:
    a) Imprecise floating point representations of real numbers.
    b) Precise representations.
    c) Valid decimal representations.
10. Integer Division type is defined by:
    a) Using the Integer Division symbol.
    b) Only using Integer variables or values in the division equation.

Chapter 5 Methods

Note: Methods cannot be defined inside other methods. They must be defined within the class definition, but outside other method definitions.

```
public class className{
        public static void main(String[] args){

        }
        public static returntype1 method1(){

        }
        public static returntype2 method2(){

        }
        public static returntype3 method3(){

        }
}
```

Designing Methods

Methods have been around for a long time and ways to build good methods have been discussed many times as well. Methods have had almost as many names as there are programming languages. You will also hear those called functions, modules, or procedures.

Methods serve several purposes in structured programming:

- They allow you to break up code into smaller coherent chunks.
- They allow you to reuse code.

- They allow you to share code easily.
- They allow you to test code separately.
- They make code easier to read and understand.

The main design goal of a method is to build a black box. A black box is an idea that has an almost identical relationship in physical design. It is an object where the inputs and output are known, but the internal workings are a mystery. The object can be swapped in and out as needed without adversely affecting the workings of the rest of the system.

In order to meet this goal, we introduce the terms, cohesion and coupling.

Cohesion is the concept that a method has one purpose and its independence from other methods. A method with one purpose is thought to be one with high cohesion, one with more than one purpose is thought to be of low cohesion. How can we tell if we have a method with high cohesion? A simple rule of thumb is to define the purpose of a method with one sentence. If that sentence cannot be stated without using the terms "and" or "or" (or any related conjunctives) you do not have a highly cohesive method.

Coupling is the concept of how any two modules communicate with each other. Coupling ranges from loosely coupled to tightly coupled. The goal here is to be loosely coupled (again think of the black box). A loosely coupled pair of modules do not have to know anything about each other to work together. It is much easier to trace the data flow between modules. To test this module all you need to do is build a driver program that fakes inputs and prints out the outputs. The different levels of coupling are:

Loose Coupling
- Calling parameters (Primitive and Reference data types)
- Function Returns (Primitive and Reference data types)
- Messaging (Message Coupling)
- Files (External Coupling).

Tight Coupling
- Global variables (static)
- Content Coupling (Accessing the local data of another module)

I would never use global variables or access the local data of another method. Global constants are fine, since they cannot change. As I mention below, I would restrict messaging and files to specialized methods.

Methods can usually be grouped into one of several types:

Control methods – These methods select from one or more options of program flow. Your main method is usually a control method. Unless it is your main, the option should be passed as a parameter or be based on the input (type of record in a file) and clearly defined.

Input/Output Methods – It is recommended that you build one method for each file/report/message queues you are reading/writing from to isolate any changes in format to that method.

Processing methods – These are known as business logic methods and will be your major methods.

During development you will probably produce two other specialty methods.

Driver methods – These are small, usually main, methods built to test methods that cannot be tested otherwise. They usually consist of the minimum number of type definitions, print statements, and method calls needed to test your code.

Stubs – these are the first version I write of a new sub method. A stub consists of little more than the method header, a set of print statements to validate the input arguments, and a valid return statement. I then fill these in as I write and validate the rest of my methods.

Methods should usually:

- Have one entrance and one exit.
- Be short and clear.
- Have a single purpose.

Method Header

Methods other than the main have a format very similar to the main method

```
public static Returntype MethodName(argument list ){
        //Variable Definition
        //code
} // end MethodName
```

All of the methods that are in our primary class
will be static.

Most methods are of security type public. We will
not talk about security in this class.

Returntype can be any single:

- primitive or
- reference type or
- void.

If you have a return type other than void, then you
must have a return (reserved word) statement
within your method with values of the same type as
your return type.

The return value is an excellent method of getting a
value back from your method.

Note: For completeness there is one special
method type that does not have a return type at all.
This is called a **class constructor**. We will not be
building these in this class. Constructors have the
following characteristics:

- They have the same name as their class.
- They are used to initialize a class.
- They have no return type.
- They are non-static

- They are invoked with the keyword new.

Your argument list consists of a set of variable type and name pairs separated by a comma. The argument list is used to pass values into a method, thus allowing you to use the same code on different values. In the case of reference data types, it is an additional method of getting information back from your method.

Your method name and argument list (types - not names) taken together must be unique within a class. The name and argument list is called a method signature. The return type is not part of the method signature. This uniqueness lets the compiler define the method name within the class. This is how Java allows more than one method with the same name to be within the same class. This is called **Polymorphism**. An Example:

```
public static int CSCIConvert.Parse(String InString, int ErrorValue)
public static double CSCIConvert.Parse(String InString, double ErrorValue)
```

These Two Parse methods belong to the CSCIConvert class. There method signatures are Parse+String+int and Parse+String+double respectively. The method signatures are different, therefore they can both reside within the same class. If I decided to add a third Parse Method

```
public static float CSCIConvert.Parse(String InString, double ErrorValue)
```

This would be illegal, since the method signature would be Parse+String+double which is the same

as one of the two existing ones. However, if I
decided to add

```
public static float CSCIConvert.Parse(String InString, float ErrorValue)
```

This would be completely legal since the method
signature is: Parse+String+float

Argument Passing

Types can be either primitive or reference.

The names used are only meaningful to the method
itself. You can call it using any name you want.
Just ensure that the type is the same.

Header examples:

```
public static boolean IsNotDouble(String TestString)
```

isNotDouble has a return value of type boolean, but
takes a String Value

```
public static int CSCIConvert.Parse(String InString, int ErrorValue)
```

Parse has a return value of type int and takes two
input values one String and the other int.

To call these, we need to define some variables:

```
final static int ERROR = 1;
String myString = "25";
boolean isTrue;
int number;
```

And then we can call them as:

```
isTrue = IsNotDouble(myString);
number = CSCIConvert.Parse(myString,ERROR);
```

You can see that I did not use the same variable names when I called the methods, as I defined them. However, I did use the same data types.

You can pass arguments in two ways, by value (primitive data types and Strings) or by reference (reference data types).

Passing by value means that value of the variable is not changed when you return from your routine. You can change the value inside the routine all you want, but when you return it is not changed. For instance: Suppose you wrote the following code:

```
int input = CSCIConvert.Parse(args[0],ERROR);
System.out.println("Before passbyValue input = " + input);
passByValue(input);
System.out.println("After passbyValue input = " + input);
```

With a method passByValue

```
public static void passByValue(int number){
        System.out.println("Entering passbyValue number = " + number);
        number = number + 1;
        System.out.println("Leaving passbyValue number = " + number);
} // end passByValue
```

If I run the program with an input of 5, It makes sense that that the first printouts say

Before passbyValue input = 5
Entering passbyValue number = 5
Leaving passbyValue number = 6

But why does input still equal 5 when number = 6?

After passbyValue input = 5

The variable input points to a different memory location than number. When a primitive value is passed into a method, a copy is made of that value and placed in a different memory location and is used by the method. If you look at the diagram below the Value is copied from memory location 1 (accessed by the calling process) to memory location (accessed by the method)

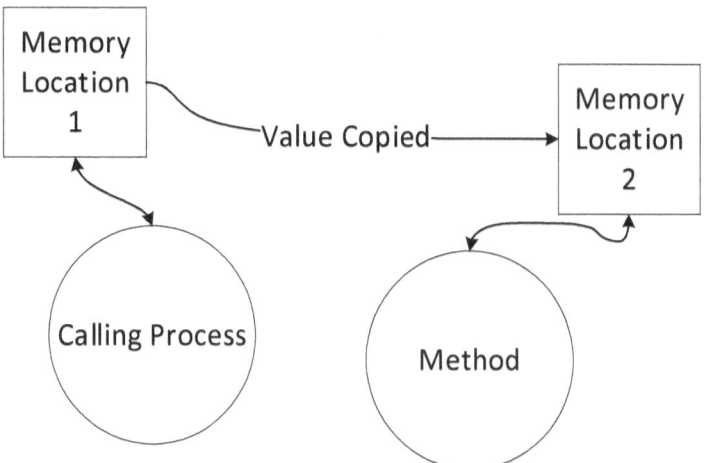

So how do you get the variables to change? This is the purpose of the return value. By setting a return type and returning that value we can set a value into either the original or a different variable. This makes it easier to follow a variable's changes.

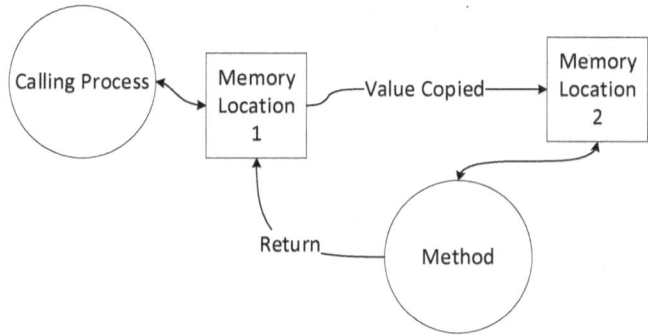

In this code the method looks very similar, all we are doing is changing the return type from void to int, and returning the modified Input. This changed program looks like:

```
int input = CSCIConvert.Parse(args[0],ERROR);
System.out.println("Before passbyValue input = " + input);
input = passByReturn(input);
System.out.println("After passbyValue input = " + input);
```

And the method

```
public static int passByReturn(int number){
        System.out.println("Entering passbyValue number = " + number);
        number = number + 1;
        System.out.println("Leaving passbyValue number = " + number);
        return number;
} // end passByReturn
```

Now our output is:

> Before passbyValue input = 5
> Entering passbyValue number = 5
> Leaving passbyValue number = 6
> After passbyValue input = 6

By using the return type, we can change the input. However, while we can pass multiple values into a

Method, we can only get one value out. Is there a different way?

The answer is reference types. Reference types are always passed by call by reference. This means that the actual memory location is passed. In our last chapter, we designed a stamp data type to hold three different data types. Let us define an even simpler one that holds a single integer, to allow us to see what pass by integer looks like:

```
public static class refint{
        public int number;
} // end refint
```

We are going to change our method to pass by reference. Notice that there is one memory location. The memory address is copied.

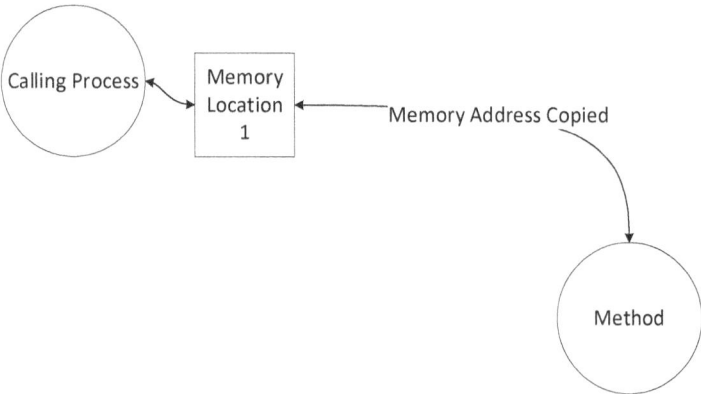

The code now looks like:

```
int input = CSCIConvert.Parse(args[0],ERROR);
System.out.println("Before passbyValue input = " + input);
input = passByReturn(input);
System.out.println("After passbyValue input = " + input);
```

And the method is very similar to passByValue

```
public static void passByRef(refint input){
        System.out.println("Entering passByRef input = " + input.number);
        input.number = input.number + 1;
        System.out.println("Leaving passByRef input = " + input.number);
        return;
} // end passByRef
```

And the results are:

Before passbyRef number = 5
Entering passByRef input = 5
Entering passByRef input = 6
After passbyRef number = 6

Calling Other Methods

Methods can call other methods. In fact when we called System.out.println() we were calling the println() method from our Add methods and our main. We called passByValue, passByReturn and passByRef from the main.

Method Body

The Method Body consists of java statements and method calls. It is everything between the two braces {}. It usually ends with the return statement. We will get into this in subsequent chapters.

Review

Methods serve several purposes:

- They allow you to break up code into smaller coherent chunks.
- They allow you to reuse code.
- They allow you to share code easily.
- They allow you to test code separately.
- They make code easier to read and understand.

Methods should have high cohesion and be loosely coupled.

Methods should
- Have one entrance and one exit.
- Be short and clear
- Have a single purpose
- Methods should pass information through calling parameters or function returns and not global variables.

Pass by value means that a copy of the value is passed into the method and the calling variable is never changed.

Pass by reference means that the memory location is passed into the method and that the calling variable can be changed.

Primitive variables and Strings are always passed by value.

Other reference variables are always passed by reference.

The argument list in a method definition includes the data type and a name that is used in the method for each parameter. Each type and name are separated by a comma. The name is only valid for the internal method. You can call it using any name you want. Just ensure that the type is the same.

The return type is included for a return. The return type can include any of:

- primitive or
- reference type or
- void.

If you have a return type other than void, you must have a return statement with a return variable of that type.

Methods can call other methods.

Two methods can have the same name as long as they have a different argument list by type.

Method calls include a variable with the same type as the type needed by the method. You do not include the type and the name does not have to be the same. The order of the types called is critical.

Questions

1. Method Headers consist of everything except:
   a) Security Type
   b) Return Type
   c) Name
   d) Optional Argument List
   e) Parentheses
   f) Brackets
2. Method Argument lists consist of everything except
   a) Data Type
   b) Name
   c) Number of Arguments
   d) Comma separating argument pairs
3. Cohesion means
   a) How modules communicate between each other.
   b) How many things a module can do.
   c) How modules are compiled.
   d) How you set your comments.
4. Well defined methods have everything except:
   a) One Entrance
   b) One Exit
   c) One Purpose
   d) One Variable.
5. The Difference between Pass by Value and Pass by Reference is:
   a) Pass by value makes a copy of the variable. Pass by reference means that the memory location is passed.
   b) Pass by reference makes a copy of the variable. Pass by value means that the memory location is
   c) There is no difference.

6. Primitive Types and Strings are always
   a) Passed by Value
   b) Passed by Reference
   c) Can be passed either way.
7. Coupling means
   a) How modules communicate between each other.
   b) How many things a module can do.
   c) How modules are compiled.
   d) How you set your comments.
8. Methods consist of:
   a) Method Header
   b) Variable definitions
   c) Code or method body.
   d) Method declarations.
   e) All of the above
9. Two distinct methods within the same class cannot have:
   a) Different names and the same argument lists.
   b) Same name and the same argument list
   c) Same name and different argument lists.
   d) Different names and different argument lists.
10. Return Values can be:
    a) void
    b) int
    c) String
    d) Boolean
    e) Any defined Reference Type
    f) All of the above

Chapter 6. Sequential Logic Structure

Basic Logic Structures

Now that we know about data and methods, we need to learn how to use them.

There are three basic logic structures in most programming languages they are sequential, decision, and loops.

We are going to go through the basic types of each in the next three chapters.

Sequential Logic Structure

The sequential logic Structure is the simplest logic structure and it is the one that is used in every other logic structure. It has three characteristics:

1. Beginning
2. End
3. Instructions that directly follow one another

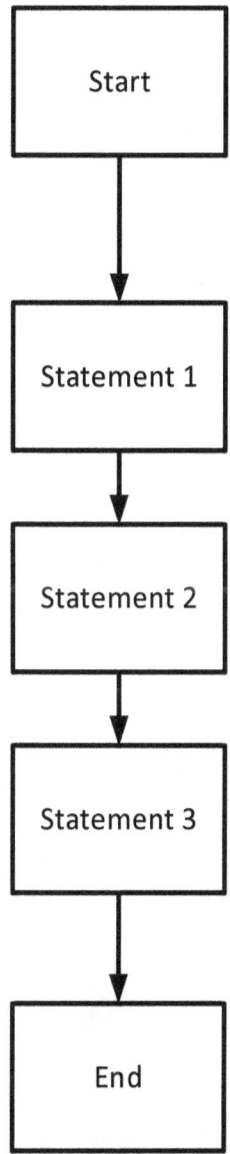

Remember: Each java statement must end in a semicolon.

So, what kind of instructions fit within this logic?

Type Declarations:

```
int anInt;
String Message;
String AString = "George Washington";
int anInt = 34;
boolean isTrue;
```

Assignment Statements:

```
myInteger = 5;
adouble = 3.45 + myInteger;
aString = "George Washington";
```

Calls to Methods:

```
System.out.println("George Washington");
```

Sequential logic includes any type of statement that does not require the other two types of logic. You can actually write small simple methods or programs just using the sequential logic structure, but you will find that you can't do anything without it.

Assignment Statements

Assignment statements are extremely important to any program. In an assignment statement you place the value on the right-hand side of the equals sign (=) into the memory location denoted by the variable of the left-hand side.

Assign a value to a primitive variable.

```
Anint = 5;
IsTrue = false;
```

Assign a memory location to a reference variable.

```
myPerson = new Person();
aString = "George Washington";
```

Move the result from an arithmetic expression, or logical expression, or a method, into a variable.

```
adouble = 3.45 + myInteger;
isTrue = (true || false);
isTrue = CSCIMath.IsNotInt(InputVar);
```

Expressions

Expressions can be looked at as the right-hand side of the assignment statement. They generally come in two types:

1. Arithmetic expressions
2. Logical expressions

Arithmetic Expressions

An Arithmetic expression is an expression that returns a numeric value. The arithmetic operators that we will use are:

+ Additive operator (also used for String concatenation)
- Subtraction operator
* Multiplication operator
/ Division operator
% Remainder operator

The order of precedence is the same as in basic mathematics:

1. parentheses (),
2. negation (-),
3. multiplication (*,/,%), and
4. addition (+, -).

You can logically put an arithmetic expression in any place that you would place a hard-coded primitive variable of the same type. They never stand alone. Examples:

```
Alpha + Beta * 3.5 / Width
3 + 4
PI  * R * R
```

Strings

Yes, you can do some arithmetic expressions with strings.

Concatenation

```
String OutputString = First + " " + Last;
```

Alternatively, you can use the concat method (I have never seen this used).

```
String OutputString = First.concat(" ");
OutputString = OutputString.concat(Last);
```

Example

```
String First = "Greg";
String Last = "Almond";
String wholeName = First + " " + Last;

Now wholeName contains "Greg Almond"
```

Separating Strings at a certain character, e.g., a comma separated value record (.csv):

```
String SYMBOL  = ",";
String SplitArray[];
Splitarray = InputString.split(SYMBOL);
```

Now SplitArray[0] has the first field up to the comma, SplitArray[1] has the second and so on.

If you had a file with a record structure consisting of name, height, and weight that looked like:

Kaden Diaz,65,242
Indigo Chaney,65,183
Harlan Hooper,71,200
Kato Mckinney,62,233
Rinah Norton,63,164

Eleanor Padilla,73,201
Quamar Ramos,66,177

You might write your record splitting code to look like:

```
String Name;
String  Height;
String Weight;
String SplitArray[];
Splitarray = InputString.split(SYMBOL);
Name = SplitArray[0];
Height = SplitArray[1];
Weight = SplitArray[2];
```

Substring (like Subtraction)

Assume that you have a set of names composed of first, middle, and last names (no titles or suffixes). These are separated by spaces. You may have multiple middle names. You need to segregate the first, middle, and last names. We are going to use indexOf, lastIndexOf, and substring to accomplish this task.

```
firstPos = name.indexOf(" ");
first = name.substring(0,firstPos);
lastPos = name.lastIndexOf(" ");
last = name.substring(lastPos+1);
middle = name.substring(firstPos+1,lastPos);
```

Logical Expressions

Logical expressions are formed by a pair of parentheses "()" which return a true or false. They never stand alone. They may be on one side of an assignment statement or they may be in an if statement (see chapter 6). Inside the parentheses is a boolean expression or equality expressions or any combination of the two.

You can put a logical expression in any place that you would place a boolean value.

There are three ways to express a logical expression (these can all be combined).

Boolean Expressions

Boolean expressions consist of one or more boolean values, true, or false, or variables (type boolean) connected by the boolean operators. Unlike arithmetical expressions, boolean expressions must be surrounded by parentheses (). The main operators are:

> "&&" for AND
> "||" for OR
> ! for NOT

(A && B) is true if A is true and B is true, otherwise it is false.

(A || B) is true if A is true and or B is true, it is false if both A and B are false.

(!(A)) is true if A is false and false if A is true.

The order of Operations is parentheses, NOT, and then left to right.

Equality Expressions

Equality expressions use the relative values of alphabetic, numeric values, or reference values to get a boolean value from them.

Note: primitive values are more straight-forward than reference values. If you try using the operators on reference values (including Strings), you will be comparing the memory location and not the value, so don't do it. I will show you the right way to do it.

Non-boolean primitive Values

The main operators are:

```
==          Equal to (two = symbols)
!=          Not equal to
>           Greater than
>=          Greater than or equal to
<           Less than
<=          Less than or equal to
```

If A and B are of the same type (no guarantees if they aren't), The basic format is:

```
(A == B)
(A != B)
(A >  B)
(A >= B)
(A <  B)
(A <= B)
```

These are just expressions and not complete statements. Be careful and do not confuse equality (==) with assignment (=). Hopefully, the compiler will catch the issue, but I will not guarantee it.

One way to ensure that the compiler will catch your error is to reverse the normal way of writing an equality statement when you are using a single variable in an equivalence statement.

If you are trying to check whether the variable Counter equals 23, instead of writing it:

```
(Counter == 23)
```

Write it as:

```
(23 == Counter)
```

Since the compiler cannot put the value of counter into the literal constant 23, it will throw an error for (23 = Counter) at compile time. Thus, avoiding countless hours of confusion and headache.

Note: Comparisons will work with char variables and there are times that this is very useful. However, you are comparing the codes and not the letters and it is case sensitive, since 'A' does not equal 'a'. So, make sure that your characters are the same case or check both cases:

```
if (('M' == inChar) || ('m' == inChar))
        system.out.println("male")
```

Reference Values

Strings and most reference values have built in comparison methods that should be used instead of the operators. These methods are:

```
.equals(a);
.compareTo(a);
```

Where you call the method from your object and a is another object of the same type.

.equals returns true if the values they hold are equivalent and false otherwise.
.compareTo returns an int denoting the relative value.

A.compareTo(B)   is 0 if they are equivalent.
> 0 if A > B
< 0 if A < B

For instance, say you have three Strings:

```
String Alpha = "George";
String Beta = "George";
String Charlie = "Sam";

Alpha.equals(Beta) would return true
Beta.equals(Alpha) would return true
Charlie.equals(Alpha) would return false
Alpha.equals(Charlie) would return false

Alpha.compareTo(Beta) returns 0
Alpha.compareTo(Charlie) returns a number < 0
Charlie.compareTo(Alpha) returns a Number > 0
```

122

To use these functions, you would build an expression like:

```
(Alpha.equals(Beta))
(Alpha.compareTo(Beta) == 0)
(Alpha.compareTo(Beta)  <  0)
(Alpha.compareTo(Beta)  >  0)
```

For Strings you can avoid the headaches of worrying about case by either converting to upper (or lower case) by using the methods toUpperCase() or toLowerCase() or by using the IgnoreCase options on the comparison methods:

```
Alpha.equalsIgnoreCase("george")
Alpha.CompareToIgnoreCase("george")
```

Would return true and 0 respectively.

Combining Expressions

Since logical expressions become boolean values, you can combine them using the boolean operators && and ||.

For instance: you could build an assignment

```
boolean Nonsense = true;
String Alpha = "Smith";
String Beta "Jones";
int Height = 15;
int Width = 52;
boolean IsItTrue ;
IsItTrue = ((Alpha.compareTo(Beta)> 0)
        && (Height > Width) || Nonsense);
```

Or it may be clearer to write the sequence as:

```
AlphavsBeta = (Alpha.compareTo(Beta)> 0)
HeightvsWidth = (Height > Width)
Combined = (AlphavsBeta && HeightvsWidth)
IsItTrue = Combined || Nonsense;
```

Which would let you check the intermediate values, if you run into problems.

Aside: I would make liberal use of parentheses to make certain that my meaning is clear.

I would also break up large expressions, by assigning them to intermediate variables, to be certain that others understand what I am saying. Breaking up expressions also helps in debugging, by allowing you to see intermediate values in a debugger or print them out.

Calls to Methods

To call a method simply use the method name followed by parentheses with variables in the same type and order as the method definition. The variable names in the calling sequence can differ from the method declaration. In the case of primitive and strings, you can substitute, hard coded values for variable names. Let us look at a few examples:

```
public static boolean IsNotInt(String test_string)
```

This method returns a boolean and is called with a String. It checks the String to see if it is an integer (a whole number), and returns true, if the input string is an integer, or false, if it is not.

Since there is only one String variable, you can call this in a couple of ways (assuming that isTrue and InputVar have been predefined and that we have set InputVar:

```
isTrue = CSCIConvert.IsNotInt(InputVar);
isTrue = CSCIConvert.IsNotInt("5");
```

Let us build a more complex method. One to print out how
old someone is:

```
public static void PrintPerson(String First, String Last, int Age){
    String OutputString = " He is " + First + " " + Last
        + " and he is " + Age + " years old";
    System.out.println(OutputString);
    return;
} //end PrintPerson
```

You can call this with

```
String One = "Uncle";
String Two = "Charley";
int  Age = 63;
PrintPerson(One, Two, Age);
```

Or You can hard code these values

```
PrintPerson("Uncle", "Charley", 63);
```

And still get the output:

He is Uncle Charlie and he is 63 Years Old.

You realize that unless you mix up the data types or add or omit one, you will not get an error. For instance, while any of these will give you a compiler error:

```
PrintPerson(One, Age, Two);
PrintPerson (Age, One, Two);
PrintPerson (One, One, Two);
PrintPerson(One, Two, , Age, Output);
```

This will not:

```
PrintPerson (Two, One, Age);
```

You will just have:

He is Charley Uncle and he is 63 Years
Old.

Another way to use methods is in an assignment
statement. For example, in java.lang.Math, there
are any number of math routines that require one or
more double arguments and return a double as a
value. For instance, say you wanted to get the
length of hypotenuse using the Pythagorean
Theorem:

```
double A, B, C;
A = 4.0;
B = 3.0;
C = sqrt(A*A + B*B);
```

C is the hypotenuse of the triangle.

Putting it together

Can we write a program using just sequential logic.
Well, we already have. Your basic DisplayName
program was a sequential logic program. Let us try
something much more complicated. Let us
combine a couple of things that we have learned so
far and figure out the hypotenuse of a triangle:

1. We will use args[] from the input to keep from hard
    coding the two sides of the triangle.
2. We will use CSCIConvert.Parse to change the
    inputs to integer.
3. We will set up constants for errors.
4. We will use sequential logic only.

5. We will use the java Math class to get the sqrt function.

Set up looks like:

```
int Height = CSCIConvert.Parse(args[0],ERROR);
int Length = CSCIConvert.Parse(args[1],ERROR);
double HeightSquared;
double LengthSquared;
double Hypotenuse;
```

And the code is:

```
HeightSquared = Height * Height;
LengthSquared = Length * Length;
Hypotenuse = Math.sqrt(HeightSquared +
LengthSquared);

System.out.println("Triangle Height = " +
        Height + " Length = " + Length +
        " Hypotenuse = " + Hypotenuse);
```

Possible results include:

```
::\java>java SequentialHypotenuse 3 4
Triangle Height = 3 Length = 4 Hypotenouse = 5.0

::\java>javac SequentialHypotenuse.java

::\java>java SequentialHypotenuse 4 5
Triangle Height = 4 Length = 5 Hypotenuse = 6.4031242374328485

::\java>java SequentialHypotenuse 4 4
Triangle Height = 4 Length = 4 Hypotenuse = 5.656854249492381

::\java>java SequentialHypotenuse a e
Triangle Height = 4 Length = 4 Hypotenuse = 5.656854249492381

::\java>java SequentialHypotenuse 3 4
Triangle Height = 3 Length = 4 Hypotenuse = 5.0
```

128

Review

There are three basic logic structures in most programming languages they are sequential, decision, and loops.

The sequential logic flow is not the most complex logic flow, it can be the simplest. However, you can do a lot with it. As you will see the other two depend on it, especially the logical expressions that we have shown you. Assignment statements and method calls will make up a considerable amount of your code.

The sequential logic structure consists of

Variable definitions

The Assignment Statement
Left-Side = Variable
Middle is "="
Right-Side
Variable or hard coded
Value.
Arithmetic or logical
Expression
Method Call
Method Call

Expressions
> Arithmetic expressions
> Logical expressions
> Boolean expression
> Equality expression
>> Primitive
>> Relational
> Combination

Questions

1. Which one is not a computer logic flow:
   a) Decision Logic
   b) Sequential Logic
   c) Random Logic
   d) Loop Logic
2. In an assignment statement, The Left-Hand Side must be:
   a) A Variable
   b) A Logical Expression
   c) Blank
   d) An Arithmetic Expression
   e) A Constant.
3. A Boolean Expression must always be surrounded by:
   a) A forest
   b) Variables
   c) Braces {}
   d) Brackets []
   e) Parentheses ()
4. If A is True and B is False, then A && B is:
   a) True
   b) False
5. If A is True and B is False then A || B is:
   a) True
   b) False
6. If A = "eagle" and B = "giraffe" then:
   a) A.compareTo(B) > 0
   b) A.compareTo(B) == 0
   c) A.compareTo(B) < 0
7. Which is true about calling a method:

a) It is important to keep the parameters in order.
b) Doesn't matter what order you have the parameters in as long as you use the same names.
c) If you have them in the wrong order the compiler will always tell you if make a mistake.
8. You can use a method call:
   a) As a separate statement.
   b) In a logical expression.
   c) In an arithmetic Expression.
   d) All of the above.
9. What happens if you use the equivalence (==) operation with a reference Variable.
   a) It compares the values
   b) It compares the memory locations.
   c) It gives you an error.
   d) Unknown.
10. (True or False) You can always assign a logical expression to a boolean variable

Chapter 7. Decision Logic

You make decisions every day, so why wouldn't a computer? After sequential logic the most used logic type is decision making. Decision logic in computer programs is used to accomplish many things, from setting values to changing the path that a computer program takes. Java has two basic forms of decision making statements (if else and switch).

If Else Logic

The basic form of the if statement is:

```
if (LogicalExpression) {
        code set a
} // end if
else {
        code set b
} // end else
```

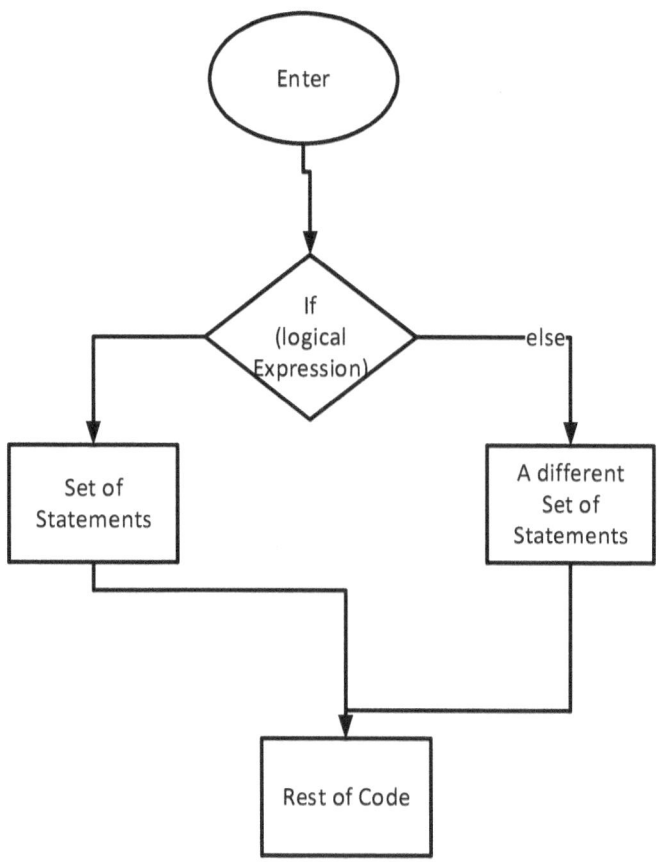

LogicalExpression is any logical expression (see chapter 5). The action statements go between the code braces. The else section is optional.

If LogicalExpression is True, then "code set a" would execute and "code set b" would be ignored. Execution would continue at the code block beginning after the //end else statement.

If LogicalExpression is False, then "code set a" would be ignored and "code set b" would execute. Execution would continue at the code block beginning after the //end else statement.

You can also eliminate the code block, if and only if, you have one statement, e.g.:

```
if (min > x) min = x;
```

However, I usually avoid doing this in case I want to add code to the if statement later. It is easier to add statements to an existing code block than to add a code block. Suppose you had a scoring program and were inputting one score at a time (poor design by the way). Scores were between 0 and 100, you might check the scores through an if else like:

```
if ((Score > 100) || (Score < 0)){
        System.out.println("Please input a grade between 0 " +
        "and 100 Score = " + Score );
        System.exit(0);
} //endif
else {
        ProcessScores(Score);
} // end else
```

Note: For complex logical expressions, you can always pull your Logical expression out from your statement and substitute a Boolean variable. This allows you to test them separate from the Decision logic. For instance:

```
isTrue = (Score > 100) || (Score < 0));
if (isTrue){
        System.out.println("Please input a grade between " +
        "0 and 100 Score = " + Score );
        System.exit(0);
} //endif
else {
        ProcessScores(Score);
}  // end else
```

Embedded If Then Logic

You can embed additional if statements entirely
within either code block. They cannot overlap.
The else goes with the if statement within that code
block.

One word of warning, when building your
expressions: It is easy to miss a value when you
are using less than and greater than. So, check all
of your logic thoroughly and check the boundaries.
For instance: Suppose you are checking ticket
prices for admission:

Seniors 65 and Above	$10
Children < 12	$ 7
Adults and Teens	$15

One way to code this properly is:

```
if (Age > 12) {
        if (Age >= 65) Price = 10;
        else Price = 15;
} // Person is not a Child
else Price = 7;
```

Suppose I slipped up and made
        Age >= 12 or

Age > 65.

Especially in the latter case, I would have some very angry seniors.

By the way, my test cases for this included Ages (12, 13, 64, 65).

```
c:\java>java Tickets 23
 Cost of Ticket for Age 23 is 15

c:\java>java Tickets 10
 Cost of Ticket for Age 10 is 7

c:\java>java Tickets 65
 Cost of Ticket for Age 65 is 10

c:\java>java Tickets 12
 Cost of Ticket for Age 12 is 7

c:\java>java Tickets 64
 Cost of Ticket for Age 64 is 15

c:\java>java Tickets 13
 Cost of Ticket for Age 13 is 15

c:\java>java Tickets 17
 Cost of Ticket for Age 17 is 15
```

Sequential Logic with if Logic

One method of using If logic with unrelated conditions is to use sequential logic. I would call these sequential if statements. These statements must be mutually exclusive. This can be identified in two ways:

> The else is not present.
> The logical expressions are not related.

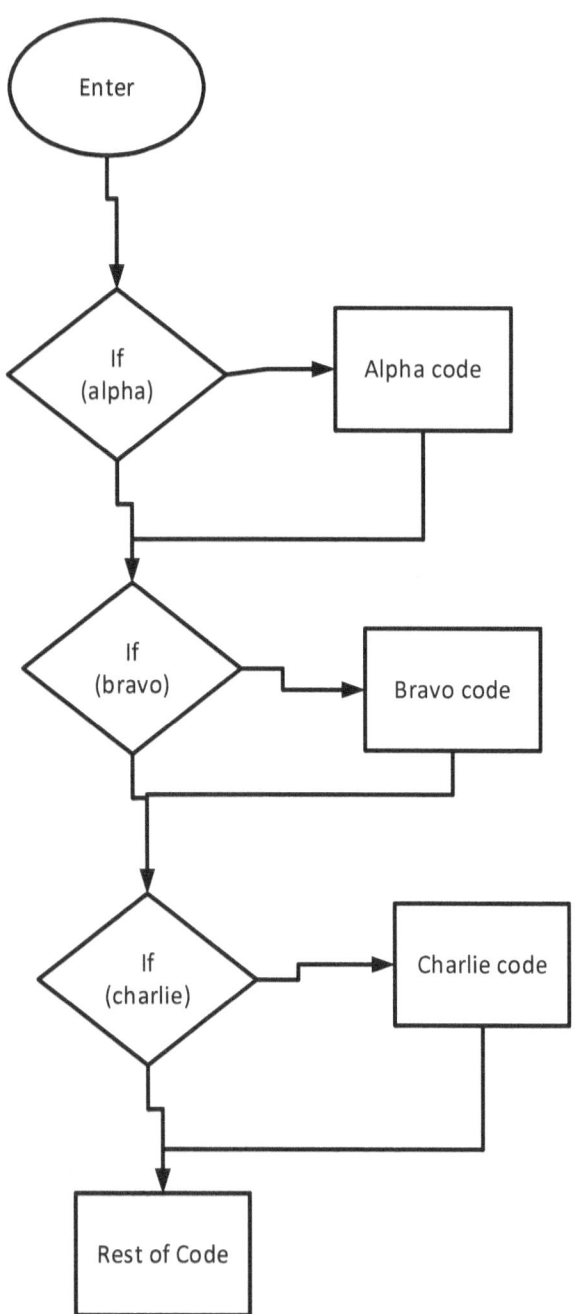

For example, let us say that you sell hamburgers with three topping, ketchup, mustard and pickles. People can order them with any combination of the three (or none). Then your logic may look like:

```
if (Ketchup) AddKetchup();
if (Mustard) AddMustard();
if (Pickles) AddPickles();
```

Case or switch Statements

Case Statements are a way of simplifying embedded if else if statements. Unlike sequential if statements, they cannot be mutually exclusive. In Java they are only useful for an int, char, or String, variable. They are less useful than they first seem. With too many cases, they become unreadable. More importantly, you have to set the values at compile time. The format is:

```
switch (SwitchVariable) {
case value1:
        step1;
        step2;
        break;
case value2:
        step1;
        step2;
        break;
default
        step1;
        step2;
        break;
} //end switch
```

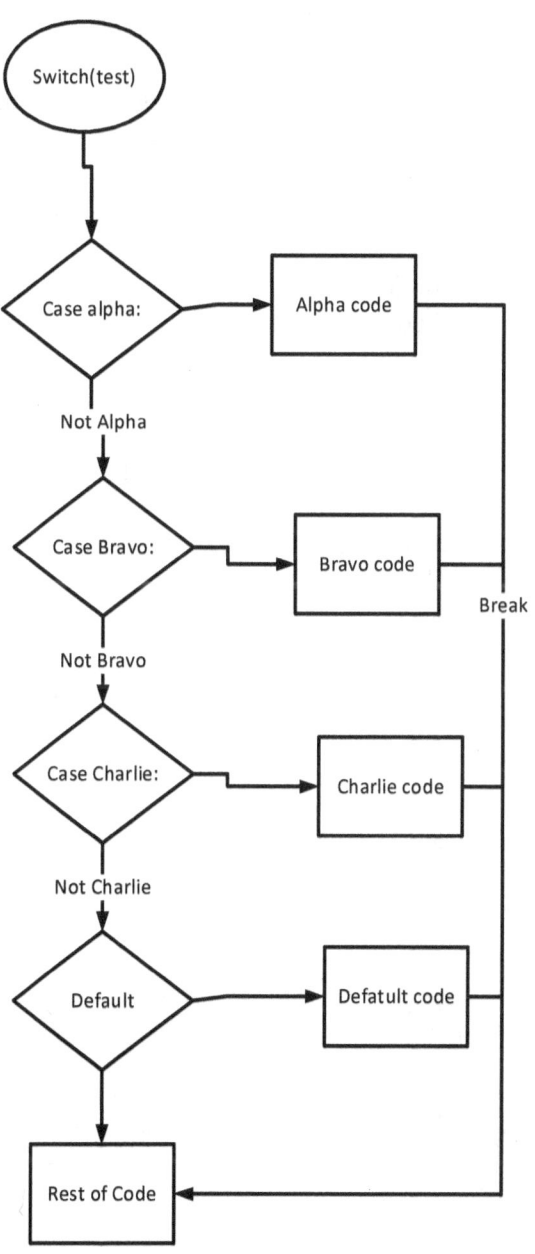

Where
switch is the switch keyword.

SwitchVariable is a variable of type int,
char, or String on which the cases depend.
case is the case keyword.
value1, value2, etc. are the individual case
values of the same type as the
SwitchVariable. (These are almost certainly
hard coded or Constants).

step1, step2 designate any valid java
statement.
break is the keyword that skips to the end of
the switch statement, without it the next
case is automatically executed whether it is
valid or not. Do not forget the break
statement.

default is the keyword for any value that is
not included in the cases.

Note: Although the standard allows the use of
String, I would not recommend using String. I
would not guarantee the results.

Example:

Where year is int and input.

```
switch (year){
        case 1:
                Grade = "Freshman";
                break;
        case 2:
                Grade = "Sophomore";
        case 3:
                Grade = "Junior";
                break;
        case 4:
                Grade = "Senior";
                break;
        default:
                Grade = "Does not compute";
                break;
} // end Switch
```

This is equivalent to:

```
if (year == 1) Grade = "Freshman";
else
        if (year == 2) Grade = "Sophomore";
        else
                if (year == 3) Grade = "Junior";
                else
                        if (year == 4) Grade = "Senior";
                                else Grade = "Does not compute";
```

Obviously, you can use multiple statements or methods in place of the single statements in either if/else logic or switch statements.

If several case statements have the same results, then you can omit the break for those statements and avoid duplicating code. For instance if you were building a simple calculator and you were letting your user input '+' for addition, '-' for subtraction, '/' for division, but 'x' for multiplication, and 'r' for remainder and you wanted to store the normal symbols. Assuming that test and oper are char and you have already converted test to lower case: you might code these requirements like:

```
switch (test){
        case '+':
                oper = '+';
                break;
        case '-':
                oper = '-';
                break;
        case '/':
                oper = '/';
                break;
        case 'x':
                oper = '*';
                break;
        case 'r':
                oper = '%';
                break;
        default;
                oper = '+';
                break;
}
```

But you might want to code the same requirements as:

```
switch (test){
        case '+':
        case '-':
        case '/':
                oper = test;
                break;
        case 'x':
                oper = '*';
                break;
        case 'r':
                oper = '%';
                break;
        default;
                oper = '+';
                break;
}
```

With the same results.

The default condition. It is always a good idea to include the default condition, unless you are guaranteed that there will never be an entry that you have not covered in your cases. Some languages will abort if you do not include the default and you get a non-specified case. Java is more forgiving. It will simply exit the switch without taking any action.

Control Methods

One major class of method is called the control method. This type of method uses decision logic in determine which method to use. This is often done by way of an input data, termed a flag. In many cases, the main is little more than a setup and control method. For instance, suppose you were conducting a study that was based on the genetic sex of the individual involved with a different set of steps for each sex. You might write a different method for each sex. The control method might look like:

```
public static void chooseTest(char Sex){
        if ((Sex == 'M') || (Sex == 'm')){
                TestProcessMale();
        } //end if Male
        else if((Sex == 'F') || (Sex == 'f'))
        {
                TestProcessFemale();
        } // end else if Female
        else
        {
                ErrorProcess();
        } // end else Error
} //end ControlMethod
```

To Test this Method, you would need at least five cases. (M, m, F, f, and some other error character).

Error Checking

Most of us have seen errors in bank accounts or bills. We like to complain about the computers. But it is usually the input data. The famous phrase Garbage in – Garbage Out (GIGO) was born.

What happens if a user inputs erroneous data. Or you are expecting an age between 0 and 100, and you get -20. Should you process it? Of course not. Therefore, you should incorporate error checking. Most error checking occurs in the data input

146

methods. Although some may be used to check the inputs to your methods.

What do you do with an error? Largely it depends how you are processing. Interactively, you might give the user a chance to correct the error. In batch processing, you would probably write the error and the erroneous entry to a log file to be corrected later. You might correct the error to a reasonable value and continue processing. This depends on your requirements.

What does error checking look like? Look at the example above. We have an integer age. It should be between 20 and 100.

```
if ((age < 20) || (age > 100)){
        // process the error
}
```

The if statement accepts any erroneous values, but allows correct values to proceed. How it processes the error depends on the requirements. It is highly probable that it would return at this point without producing a valid output.

Where does the error checking go? I usually place my error checking at the beginning of my methods.

We will learn different methods of error checking in chapter 9.

Final Thoughts

A few final thoughts on decision logic:

Decision logic code can become extremely unwieldy and complex, especially over time as additional requirements are added and expanded. Old ones are never removed even though they become obsolete and sometimes actually conflict. How do you combat this?

- You can break up your logic into smaller pieces. If a decision is not related do not keep it in the same logic flow.
- Break your logical expressions into assignment statements outside of your if/else statements. Use boolean variables.
- Break the logic up into separate methods to simplify testing. Use control methods.
- See if the logic can be rewritten to make it less cumbersome.
- Ask for help.
- If requirements conflict, alert your bosses and customers. They may not be aware that there are problems.

Testing

The only time to ensure that your logic flow is tested is during unit testing. This is where you can build test data that will test every branch and flow and especially the errors.

Review

So far, we have looked at sequential and decision logic. Decision logic is extremely powerful and complex. You need to be very careful and test all possible conditions. You need to consider improbable cases, and when you have multiple cases, for efficiency, you need to consider the likely hood of each case. You need to be very careful of a few things when writing decision logic:

- Is it readable and maintainable?
- Did I consider ever test possibility?
- Did I ensure that I missed any possible cases?
- Did I test my end and middle conditions?

The two main structures for Decision Logic in Java are:

1. if else
2. switch case

These structures depend on logical expressions which we discussed in the sequential logic chapter.

One of the main methods using this logic is the control method which is used to control your program.

Error Checking is a method of preventing user errors from creeping into your code. User input should always be checked for accuracy. It is usually a good idea to check critical inputs in methods as well.

Testing is critical of end and middle conditions are critical for decision logic. Unit testing is the best time to check your decision logic.

Questions

1. Logical Expressions are made up of:
   a) Boolean expressions
   b) Equality expressions
   c) Methods with boolean return types
   d) All of the above
2. In an if() statement what goes between the parentheses?
   a) Any int, char, or string variable
   b) A logical expression
   c) An arithmetic expression
   d) None of the above
3. In a switch() statement what goes between the parentheses?
   a) Any int, char, or string variable
   b) A logical expression
   c) An arithmetic expression
   d) None of the above.
4. Where does the else statement go in sequential decision logic
   a) At the bottom
   b) Between each if statement
   c) Nowhere
5. What is a Control Method?
   a) A method that uses a flag variable and decision logic to decide which method or methods to execute.
   b) A method that has OCD issues.
   c) A method that operates a controller.
   d) A method that processes control data.

6. Which statement is true about a break in a case statement?
   a) It serves no purpose.
   b) It tells us when the case ends.
   c) Without it the code would automatically execute the next case.
7. In embedded if else statements the else belongs to
   a) The nearest if statement within the same code block.
   b) The top if.
   c) The last else.
8. What can you do if your decision logic gets too complex?
   a) Break it up into smaller pieces or modules
   b) Look at the logic and see if it can be rewritten
   c) Ask for help
   d) All of the above
9. What happens if you use a switch statement with four possible situations and a fifth one enters, and you forgot to have a default condition?
   a) One of the first four runs at random.
   b) The first condition runs.
   c) The default condition runs.
   d) The switch exits without executing any option.
   e) An error occurs – you get fired.
10. What happens if you use a case statement with four possible situations and a fifth one enters, and you had a default condition?
   a) One of the first four runs at random.
   b) The first condition runs.
   c) The default condition runs.
   d) The switch exits without executing any option.
   e) An error occurs – you get fired.

Chapter 8. Looping

Looping is the last type of computing logic that we will look at. It uses decision logic and sequential logic, but adds the ability of code to repeat itself. Without this ability code, would be much longer, harder to understand, and take much longer to write and debug. Loops have three things in common and one major risk. The three commonalities are:

1. Start condition. Whatever condition they check must be initialized.
2. End condition. What breaks the loop.
3. Looping step.

The major risk in any loop is an infinite loop or a loop that never ends. You must ensure, when designing, coding, and testing a loop, that it has a valid end condition.

There are 4 basic Loop formations:

1. do while aka repeat until in other languages.
2. while loop
3. for aka do (not the same as a do while) aka counting loop.
4. recursion

While almost any loop can be simulated with any other loop, they each serve a specific purpose or benefit.

Do While Loop

do while loops have two basic characteristics.

1. The condition is always tested last.
2. The code is always executed at least once.

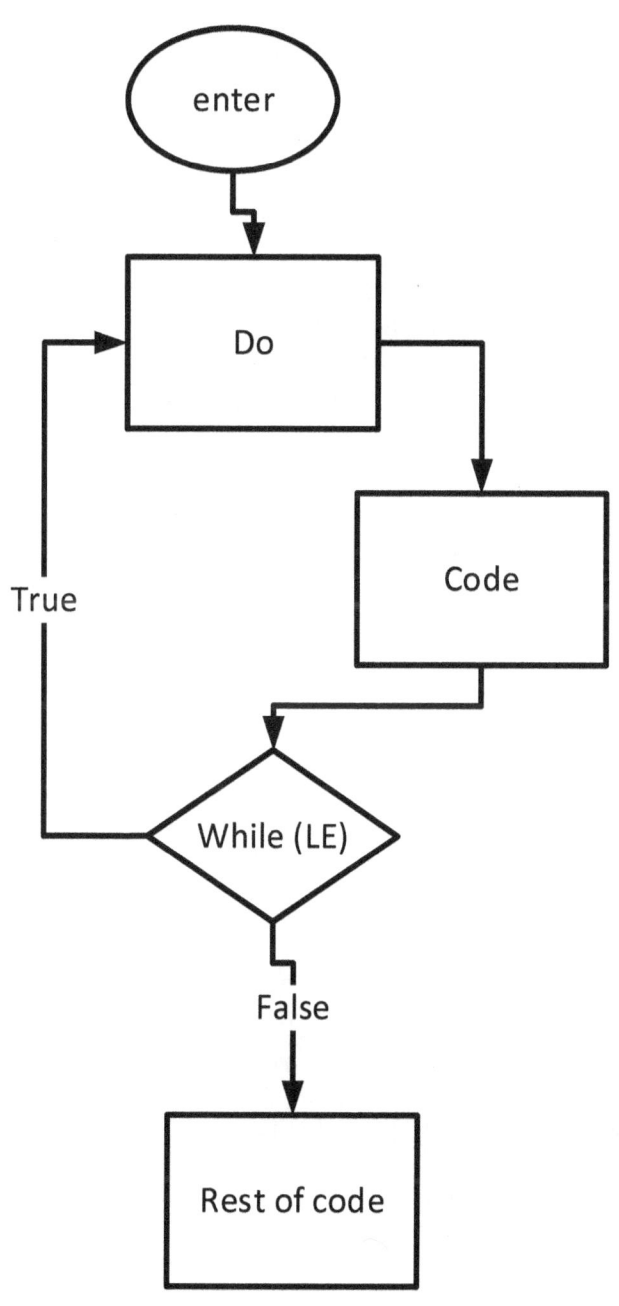

The format of a do while statement is:

```
do{
        code
} while(Logical Expression);
```

Where code consists of the statements that you want to accomplish. Let us examine a code fragment that Takes a set of integers in an array and sums them. You might write the do/while loop as:

```
int size = intArray.length
int i = 0;
int sum = 0;
do {
        sum = intArray[i];
        ++i;
} while (i < size);
```

While Loop

The while Loop is similar to the do while loop.

```
while (Logical Expression) {
        code
}  // end while
```

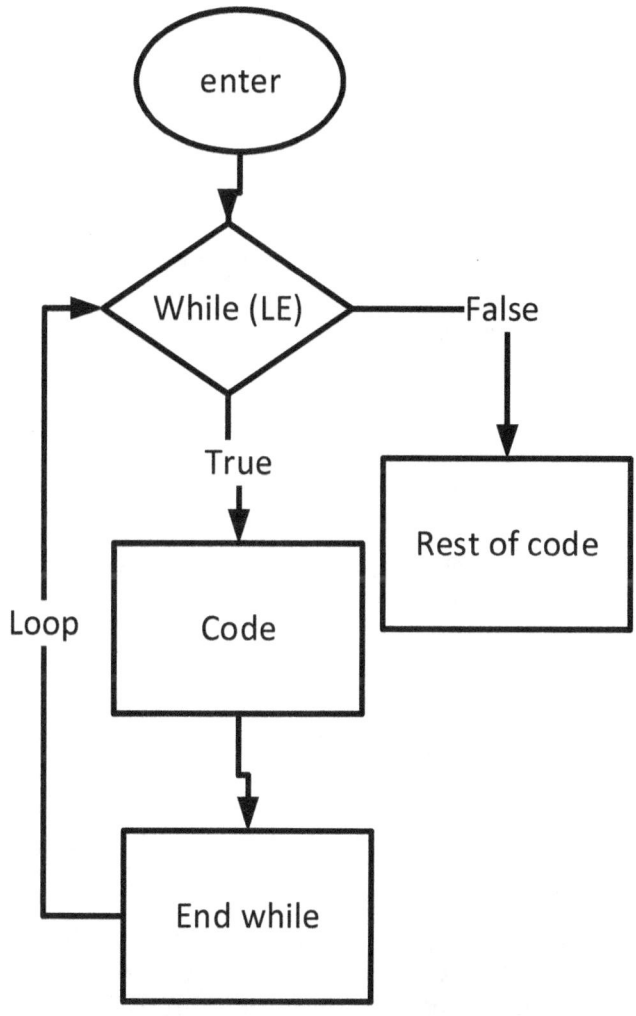

In fact, the two can be switched back and forth with a minor fix to the logical expression. The choice between the two is usually a matter of personal preference: The while loop has three basic characteristics:

1. The condition is tested first.
2. The code may not be executed at all.
3. You may need a primer read to predefine the condition.

A primer read is an initial read of the data that allows you to set up the initial condition for the loop. This lets you place the next read at the end of the loop.

In this case we do not need a primer read, the same problem we discussed in the do while looks like:

```
int size = intArray.length
int i = 0;
int sum = 0;
while (i < size){
        sum = intArray[i];
        ++i;
}
```

As you can see there really isn't much difference between the two types of loops. They are both readable, they both accomplish the same thing, and the differences are very minor. In my opinion, it is a largely a matter of taste, comfort, style, or company standards, as to which loop one would use. However, I would be consistent in my choice once I make one.

For loops

These are also called counting loops. The main purpose of for loops is to increment or decrement for a variable. For loops need three things:

1. Initialization
2. End condition
3. Increment or decrement

The basic structure is

```
for (initialization; end condition; increment){
        code
} // end for
```

The diagram for a basic for loop is the same as a while loop. Set up your initialization before you enter the loop. You add the increment before while statement. The end condition becomes your while condition.

Say you wanted to sum from 1 to 10 by 1, you might write this as:

```
for( int i = 1;  i < 11;  ++1){
        sum = sum + i;
} // end for
```

There are several things to note:

- The i variable is only valid within the for loop code block.
- The loop runs from each value of i from 1 to 10.

- The sum must be defined and initialized outside of the for loop.

You can easily reverse a for loop by reversing the beginning and end conditions and using a decrement condition. (be very careful):

```
for (int i = 10; i > 0; --i){
        System.out.println("Countdown " + i)
}
```

Will produce a countdown from 10 to 1.

Note: You can do a lot of tricks with the end condition and the increment, I feel that this is beyond this course and I don't use them, so I will not delve into these.

The problem that we looked at with the do-while and while loops looks like

```
int size = intArray.length
int sum = 0;
for(int i = 0; i < size; ++i){
        sum = intArray[i];
}
```

A final thought on these three types of loops. Any loop type can be used to simulate any other type. But it is cleaner to use a for loop when you need an incrementing loop and a while or do while loop when you need a loop that has an unknown number of iterations.

Embedded Loops

Just like decision logic, you can embed any kind of
a loop completely within any other kind of loop.
Note: I said completely. It must reside within the
code block. A couple of thoughts and or warnings.

The inner loop will execute once for every time the
outer block executes. In other words, suppose your
inner block executes 10 times each time it runs.
And your outer block executes 20 times.
Therefore, your inner block runs 20 * 10 = 200
times. So, if you don't have efficient code inside
this inner block, your program can drag.
If you make a mistake and do not initialize your
variables, you can get weird results. Say you are
dependent on a variable A starting at one in your
inner loop and you do not initialize it and by the
end of your loop it has the value of 10. The second
time through it goes from 10 to 21, the third time
from 21 to 32 and so on. Make sure you are
getting the results that you desire.

Example: We have a preloaded 2 dimensional gray
scale image array, image[][]. It is one million
pixels (1000 x 1000). It is extremely dim, so we
want to brighten it, so we want to double the
brightness of each pixel.

```
for(int j = 0; j < LENGTH; ++j){
        for(int i = 0; i < WIDTH; ++i){
                image[i][j] = 2 x image[i][j];
        }
}
```

Loading data

When loading data from a sequential file, I invariably use a while loop with a primer read. I also load it into a String ArrayList. The code may look like:

```
input = myFile.Read();
while(input != null){
        records.add(input);
        input = myFile.Read();
}
myFile.close()
```

This code works for two reasons. The Read method returns a new String whenever it returns, and it returns a null String when it reaches the end of file.

You can then process the data in the records ArrayList any way you choose.

For instance, say your file was a comma separated value (csv) file holding name and age.

You might define an internal class like:

```
public static class person{
        String name;
        int age;
}
```

You could then define an array list

```
ArrayList <person> People;
```

You could then define a decode method

```
public static ArrayList <person> decode(ArrayList<String> records){
        int ERROR = 0;
        int size = records.size();
        String line;
        String[] list;
        person newPerson;
        ArrayList <person> people = new ArrayList <person>();
        for (int i = 0; i < size ; ++i){
                line = records.get(i);
                list = line.split(",");
                newPerson = new person();
                newPerson.name = list[0];
                newPerson.age = CSCIConvert.Parse(list[1],ERROR);
                people.add(newPerson);
        }
        return people;
}
```

Note: This assumes that all your data is good.
You create a new Person in your loop so that you
do not duplicate any of your data.
You could do a similar solution with parallel
arrays.

```
int size = records.size();
String[] names = String[size];
int[] age = int[size];
public static void decode(ArrayList<String> records, String[] names, int[] age){
        int ERROR = 0;
        int size = records.size();
        String line;
        String[] list;
        for (int i = 0; i < size ; ++i){
                line = records.get(i);
                list = line.split(",");
                names[i] = list[0];
                age[i] = CSCIConvert.Parse(list[1],ERROR);
        }
        return;
}
```

names and age are passed by reference through the
command line. Now of course you need to
maintain the relationship between names and age.

You could also keep your data as String using a
two-dimensional array.

```
public static String[][] decode(ArrayList<String> records){
        int size = records.size();
        String[][] person = String[2][size]
        String line;
        String[] list;
        for (int i = 0; i < size ; ++i){
                line = records.get(i);
                list = line.split(",");
                person[0][i] = list[0];
                person[1][i] = list[1];
        }
        return;
}
```

Of course, in this last case every time you want to
access your age you need to convert it to int.

```
age = CSCIConvert.Parse(person[1][i],ERROR);
```

Now imagine that your records are getting more
complex (or that your users decide to change them,
later, by adding or deleting fields). I believe that
you would have to agree that building a class is by
far the best solution.

Recursion

The fourth type of looping is recursion. Recursion
is an interesting topic. On one hand it is a difficult
idea to get across, on the other hand once you get
the idea of recursion, the code is very simple. Some
people don't consider this a type of looping, but I
do not see any other way to categorize it.

Recursion is defined as a method calling itself. The internal call uses a different parameter. There are many examples of recursion, and most recursive algorithms can also be done in an iterative manner. The iterative solution is often more efficient. The neatest thing about recursion is the elegance and simplicity of the solution. For recursion to work, you need two things:

1. An end condition to avoid the infinite loop.
2. A method call that defines the recursion.

A very simple example (and an efficient one) is factorials. A factorial N! is a mathematical formula used in statistics to determine the relative probability of a set of choices remaining after one has been removed. The basic example used is a baseball team. You start with 9 players, you choose the pitcher, which leaves 8 players. You select the catcher that leaves 7 players, until you are left with 1 player for right field. The formula is:

$$N! = N * (N-1) * (N-2) *... 1$$

So, the recursive code becomes:

```
public static double RecursiveFactorial(int n){
if (n <= 1) return 1;
return n * RecursiveFactorial(n - 1);
} // end RecursiveFactorial
```

And if you wanted to find out how many options you had to select your team; you call it from your main routine with:

```
NFactorial =  RecursiveFactorial(9);
```

And it would quickly return 36,2880.

These numbers become very large very quickly which is why I chose double as my return code.

How does the recursive code work?

Let us assume an input of 4.

```
Call 1 RecursiveFactorial(4)
        4 is Larger than 1
        So it Runs 4 * RecursiveFactorial(3)

Call 2 RecursiveFactorial(3)
        3 is Larger than 1
So it Runs 3 * RecursiveFactorial(2)

Call 3 RecursiveFactorial(2)
        2 is Larger than 1
        So it runs 2 * RecursiveFactorial(1)

Call 4 RecursiveFactorial(1)
        1 is not larger than 1 so it returns 1 to Call 3
Call 3
        Return 2 * 1 to Call 2
Call 2
        Return 3 * 2 to Call 1
Call 1
        Return 4*6 to main

Main receives 24.
```

This is why this is called single threaded recursion.

As another example, Fibonacci numbers are double threaded recursion. The formula for Fibonacci numbers are:

```
F(0) = 0
F(1) = 1
F(n) = n-1  +  n -2
```

Thus, the recursive algorithm is:

```
public static double RecursiveFibonacci(int n){
if (n < 1) return 0;
if (n < 2) return 1;
return RecursiveFibonacci(n -1) +
        RecursiveFibonacci(n - 2);
} // end RecursiveFibonacci
```

Since you have to go down the same calling sequence for each of the two paths in the RecursiveFibonacci Sequence, this algorithm is much less efficient than the iterative solution. In fact, on my computer, while the iterative solution takes less than a second to return consistently, at an input of 45 the recursive solution takes about 7 seconds. At numbers not much higher, it refuses to return. Let us look at Fibonacci Recursion for a small Value, say 5. For Simplicity, our method is called RF().

F(5) calls RF(5) which calls R(4) + RF(3)

RF(4) calls RF(3) + RF(2)

RF(3) calls RF(2) + RF(1)

RF(2) returns 1

RF(1) returns 1

RF(3) = 1+1 returns 2

RF(2) second call returns 1

RF(4) = 2 + 1 returns 3

Meanwhile

RF(3) second call calls RF(2) + RF(1)
RF(2) third call Returns 1

RF(1) second call returns 1

RF(3) second call returns 1+1 returns 2

Finally RF(5) returns 3 + 2 = 5

Summation
RF(5) was called once.
RF(4) was called once.
RF(3) was called twice.
RF(2) was called 3 times.
RF(1) was called twice.

In an iterative solution. Each method call value
would be called once and only once and the return

value would be stored. Thus, saving significant time.

It is often quite a bit cheaper, from a runtime perspective, to turn a recursive process into a non-recursive loop.

There are languages, such as Lisp, based entirely on the recursive model. Currently, these are also known as Functional Languages and are very popular with parallel processing systems. In systems with high numbers of parallel processors, the duplicated calls are not an issue. In fact, the simplicity of code can end up with fewer errors.

Strings

Strings. There are a couple of times where you want to break up a String into its component array of characters and act on each character separately. For instance. I have found no other method to reverse the string or to remove special characters.

One fun problem is to find out if a given String is a palindrome. A palindrome is a word or phrase that once you remove all capitols and on-letters (a-z) reads the same backwards and forwards. Some examples of palindromes include:

> Don't nod.
> I did, did I?
> My gym
> Red rum, sir, is murder
> Step on no pets
> Top spot

Was it a cat I saw?

Eva, can I see bees in a cave?

No lemon, no melon

So, the basic algorithm to test if a given string is a palindrome is to:

1. Convert the string to lower (or upper case).
2. Remove all non-letters.
3. Make an inverse copy.
4. Compare the two.
5. If they are equal – you have a palindrome.

Your main logic would look like (using equals since both strings are lowercase):

```
String mainString = input.toLowerCase();
String reverseString;

mainString = removeSpecialChar(mainString);
reverseString = getReverse(mainstring);
if (mainString.equals(reverseString)){
        System.out.println(input + " is a palindrome");
}
else{
        System.out.println(input + " is not a palindrome");
}
```

The Remove Special character code uses the .toCharArrray method and then builds the String char by char. There is a char toString method, but it does not give the results that you would expect.

```
public static String removeSpecialchar(String input){
      char[] myChar;
      String test = "";
      int size = input.length();
      myChar = input.toCharArray();
      for (int i = 0; i < size; ++i){
            if ((myChar[i] >= 'a') && (myChar[i]) <= 'z'){
                  test = test + myChar[i];
            }
      }
      return test;
}
```

Finally, the getReverse method reverses the array.

```
public static String getReverse(String input){
      char[] myChar;
      String reverse = "";
      int size = input.length();
      myChar = input.toCharArray();
      for (int i = size-1; i > -1; --i){
            {
                        reverse = reverse + myChar[i];
            }
      }
      return reverse;
}
```

Review

This chapter concludes our discussion of the three forms of computer logic: sequential, decision, and looping. As you have seen, loop logic depends on both decision and sequential logic. Decision logic depends on sequential logic. Without all three we have long, cumbersome, unreadable code.

I introduced the four looping types and one new data type. The four looping types are:

1. do while
2. while
3. for
4. recursion

Most people probably would not include recursion as a type of looping and it does not have a code instruction in Java, but it is an important logic structure. If you become used to it, it has all of the attributes of a loop.

All loops have the following characteristics:

- Start condition. Whatever condition they check must be initialized.
- End condition. This breaks the loop.
- Looping step.

The do while and while loops are extremely useful when you are faced with any situation where you need to loop through something until the situation changes. What they refer to as a state change. You do not know how many times you will loop; it could be zero, it could be once, it could be 10,000 times. Obviously, if you might never loop through it, don't choose the do while loop. In this class, you will usually use one of these two when loading data, since you have no idea how much data you have.

A for loop however is used when you know how many times and by what increment you want to go through something. Running through arrays, is an obvious use of the for loops.

Recursion is a method calling a method by the same name with different parameters. The loop ends by encountering an end condition within the method.

The biggest risk with loops is infinite loops which never terminate.

Questions

1. Loops rely on
   a) Sequential logic
   b) Decision logic
   c) End conditions
   d) Looping step
   e) All of the above
2. Java Loops include all but
   a) do while
   b) repeat until
   c) for
   d) while
3. (True or False) Recursion is always more efficient than iteration.
4. Java for loops require
   a) (variable declaration; end condition; increment)
   b) (increment; end condition; variable declaration)
   c) (variable declaration; increment; end condition)
   d) (end condition; variable declaration; increment)
5. One of the differences between do while loops and while loops is:
   a) while loops always execute once and do while loops may not execute their code.
   b) do while loops always execute once and while loops may not execute their code.
   c) There is no difference.
6. (True or False) You cannot simulate any of the loops using any of the other loops:
7. Recursion consists of:
   a) A while loop calling a do while loop.
   b) A process calling itself until it encounters an end condition.

    c) A String function that reverses the letters in the string.
8. (True or False) It is best to always use the for loop to load data.
9. The biggest risk in looping is:
    a) An infinite loop.
    b) A recursive loop.
    c) A for loop with an embedded while loop.
    d) A while loop with an embedded for loop.
10. When you embed loops, you must make doubly sure that your:
    a) Variables are correctly initialized.
    b) Loops do not overlap.
    c) Logic is correct
    d) Inner loop is efficient.
    e) All of the above.

Chapter 9. Object Oriented Programming

Object Oriented programming (OOP) is based on the premise that you can define a problem as a set of objects. These objects have things that define them, called attributes. These objects can act through methods. We have looked at attributes and methods in previous chapters.

The object-oriented model has four important principles that we will explore:

1. Encapsulation
2. Polymorphism
3. Inheritance
4. Abstraction

Encapsulation is the creation of self-contained modules that show tight cohesion and low coupling.

Polymorphism is the ability to use the same name in two (or more) methods to take the same action in different ways.

Inheritance is the ability to build a child from a parent that takes on the attributes and methods of the parents and adds attributes and methods of its own. It also may alter the methods of the parent.

Abstraction is the ability to hide the implementation details and showing only the functionality to the user. This is also used to build classes that have only the interfaces defined and none of the actual bodies of the methods.

Packages

In this portion of the book. We will be building classes that are not related to the main class. These classes must be in a file with the same name as the class themselves. They should be kept in a package of their own.

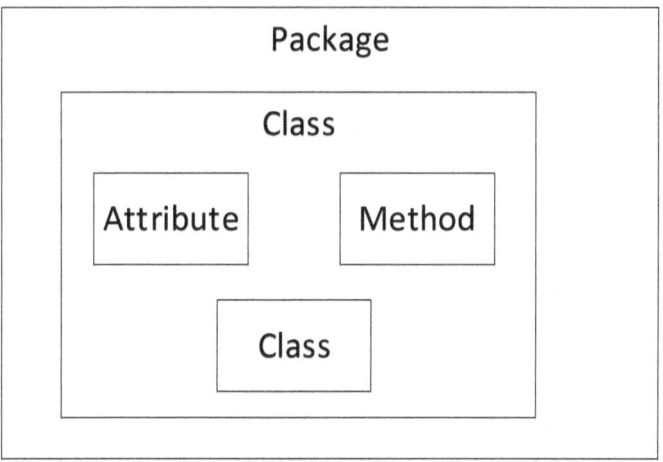

For simplicity, the classes that we will discuss will be kept in one of two packages. Classes built for the flash drive (utility classes) will be kept in CSCI. Personal classes will be kept in GBlood. I recommend that if you build them you use your first initial, last name.

So, the first statement in utility classes is:

```
package CSCI;
```

And for personal classes is:

```
package GBlood;
```

CSCI classes are kept in the directory \CSCI and GBlood classes are kept in the directory \GBlood.

To use classes from these packages you need the import statements in your code:

```
import CSCI.*;
import GBlood.*;
```

You can place these directories anyplace on you drive as long as you set up your CLASSPATH variable. Currently it is set up so that they must be set up directly under your main javauser directory on the flashdrive.

Class

In java, classes are the blueprints for your objects. We have created a number of main classes, e.g.,

```
public class HelloWorld{
        public static void main(String[] args){
                System.out.println("Hello World");
        }
}
```

And several small static classes, e.g.,

178

```
public static class nameAge{
        public String name;
        public int age;
}
```

We learned that the main class had to reside in a file with the same name (case dependent) as the class. We also learned that the static class was a template for the object. That we had to instantiate the object to bring it to life using the keyword new.

```
nameAge mynameAge = new nameAge();
```

These static classes that we built only had attributes. They did not have any methods. To turn this into an independent class is to move it to a file in \GBlood\person.java and get rid of the static keyword.

```
public class nameAge{
        public String name;
        public int age;
}
```

Now we might want to add some methods to it. For now, let us limit ourselves to add toString. toString is a common method that returns a String with the contents of an object. The default version is not very useful, since it gives us the memory location, so we want to write our own, this is called overwriting the parent version (we will learn more about this later).

```
public class nameAge{
        public String name;
        public int age;

        public String toString(){
                String format = "%-20s  %3d";
                String line = String.format(format,name,age);
                return line;
        }
```

The driver to test this class is very simple. It looks like:

```
public static void main(String[] args){
        nameAge me = new nameAge();
        me.age = 60;
        me.name = "Glen Blood";
        System.out.println(me.toString());
}
```

Constructors

Constructors are special methods that initialize the object.

Constructors have the same name as the class, have no return codes, and are only called with the new keyword.

If your parent does not define a constructor. You do not have to write your own. You can use the default constructor that is generated by the compiler.

If your parent has written any constructors then you must provide at least one constructor that uses the super() keyword to access it as the first term in your constructor. Say your parent x had a constructor x(int i). If your class xy extends x, then your constructor xy(int j) would include the term super(j) as its first statement.

So, let us add a constructor that allows us to set our data to our new class.

```
public class nameAge{
        public String name;
        public int age;

        public nameAge(){
                name = "";
                age = 0;
        }

        public nameAge(String n, int a ){
                this();
                name = n;
                age = a;
        }

        public String toString(){
                String format = "%-20s  %3d";
                String line = String.format(format,name,age);
                return line;
        }
}
```

This means that out driver can now be changed to:

```
public static void main(String[] args){
        nameAge me = new nameAge("Glen Blood",60);
        System.out.println(me.toString());
}
```

Exception Handling

We learned about using the if statement to provide one method of error checking. OOP provides us with a different spin on error checking.

OOP prefers to call this exception handing. While some practitioners believe that it replaces the if() method of checking errors, I look on them as working in tandem.

Exceptions are the OOP term for recoverable errors. Exceptions can include some system errors, e.g., file systems, as well as user errors.

Errors are reserved for non-recoverable errors like system crashes.

The exception class is java.lang.Exception

All exceptions extend this class. However the exceptions, may be found anywhere. For instance, IOException is found in the java.io package. If you are using a class, it will tell you what exceptions it throws.

To handle an exception, you use the try-catch-finally keywords.

Without a Finally block, if an exception is found anywhere in the try block, the code immediately jumps to the relevant catch block and leaves the method. If not then the rest of the code is executed.

If there is a finally section, then the same activity happens except that after the try or catch blocks finish, the finally block is executed.

For example, in CSCIConvert.Parse(String,int), I used the try on the Integer.parseInt() method an tried to catch the NumberFormatException error.

```
try{
        myValue = Integer.parseInt(InString);
        return myValue;
}
catch(NumberFormatException e){
        return ErrorValue;
}
```

If the error is caught, I returned the ErrorValue.

The way this works is the try{} attempts the code within the block and if an exception is encountered it throws the exception.

The exception then looks for a corresponding catch(){} block. If one is found, that block and only that block is executed. If there is more than one catch block for that exception, the first one that satisfies the condition is used. If no catch(){} block satisfies the exception, then the exception is elevated to the parent calling method until it reaches the main method. If the exception is still not handled, then the program aborts (a bad thing).

If there is no exception, then processing continues as though there were no catch blocks present.

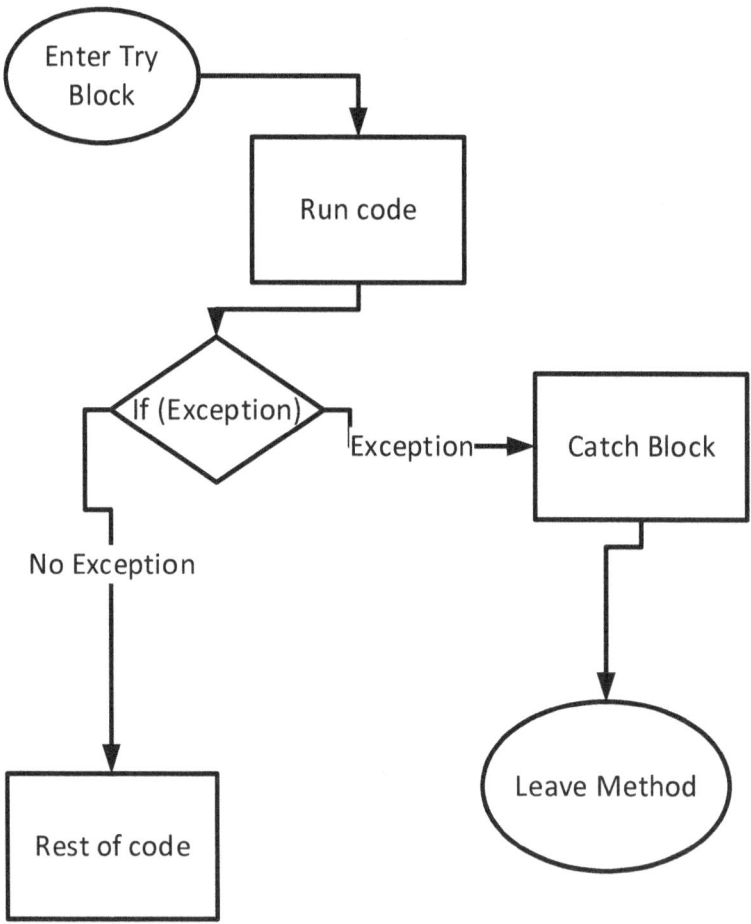

If there is a finally{} block present. This block is
executed whether a caught exception occurs or
execution happens normally. If an exception
occurs and is not ever caught, i.e., the program
terminated because you never caught the exception,
then the finally block is not executed.

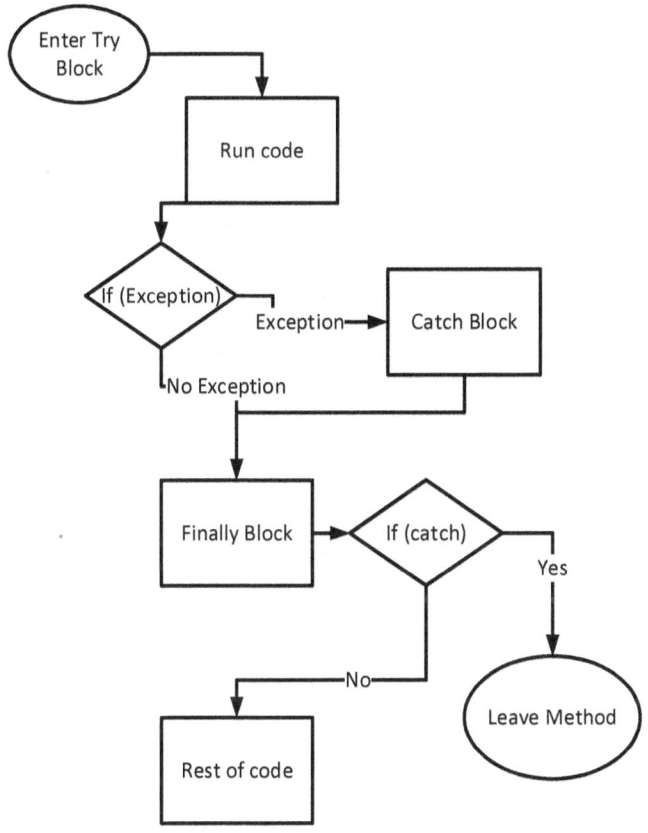

If a class throws an exception, the compiler will often force you to use a try-catch block. Use of the finally block is always optional.

You can also build your own exceptions to replace the other methods of error checking. You can also force an exception condition to occur for testing.

> Code enters try block
> > Executes each piece of code
> > > If Exception skip to catch block

If not continue to next piece
of code until try Try Block
Ends
Catch Block
Entered only on exception
Execute block code
If no finally block then end method.
If finally enter Finally Block
End Catch Block
Finally Block
Entered whether or not an Exception
happens
Execute block code
If there was an exception end block
If no Exception continue execution
End Finally block

You can have as many catch blocks as you need.
There is a generic Exception code that will let you
catch all exceptions (catch (Exception e)).

Review

Object-oriented programming is a different way of looking at design that relies on classes as the blueprints for our designs and objects for that bring them to life. The term that we use for bringing classes to life is instantiation.

Classes are kept in packages. Our class package is CSCI. Our standard for personal packages is first initial (capitalized) Last name (first letter capitalized), therefore, my package is GBlood.

Any class in package xyz must have the statement "package xyz" as its first line. Any class that uses a class from that package must use the statement "import xyz.*" before the class definition.

The class definition is "public class class name{}" with the body of the class between the braces.

This xyz class must belong to a file named xyz.java

Classes may contain any number of attributes (aka variables) methods or static classes. They set aside memory for the object and usually set initial values for the attributes.

The constructor method for a class is executed to instantiate the class. It is the only method that does not have a return value or void. It has the same name as the class. To execute them you use the "new" keyword. The default constructor has no attributes, but other constructors may have attributes, just like any other method. So xys' default constructor definition is "public xyz(){}"

with the body of the constructor between the code braces.

Constructors may be simple or complex. To instantiate a class it is required to declare the type and use the constructor as

```
xyz myObject = new xyz();
```

Exceptions and the try{}catch(){}finally{} blocks are the OOP methodology for exception handling. I believe that they augment and do not replace the older method of error checking/prevention.

Questions

1. The main blueprint of OOP is a/an
   a) Class.
   b) Object
   c) Package
   d) Method
2. Classes may be composed of:
   a) Attributes
   b) Methods
   c) Classes
   d) Objects
   e) All of the above
3. Packages may be composed of:
   a) Attributes
   b) Methods
   c) Classes
   d) Objects
   e) All of the above
4. Constructors are used to:
   a) Build buildings.
   b) Set aside memory for an object.
   c) Initialize values for an object's attributes.
   d) Two of the above.
5. The default constructor is provided by:
   a) Ada Lovelace.
   b) The parent of the class.
   c) The Java compiler.
   d) You always have to write a constructor.
6. If the parent class has a non-default constructor, then:
   a) You have to provide a non-default constructor with the same attributes.
   b) You have to provide a constructor that activates the parent's constructor in it.
   c) You can rely on Java's default constructor.

7. In a non-static or external class that class:
   a) Can be in a file with all of the other classes in the package.
   b) Must be in its own file classname.java.
   c) May be in a compiled java library before it is used.
   d) Does not exist.
8. A physical package is:
   a) A file containing related classes.
   b) A file system folder containing class source code and/or java binary's.
   c) Something from the liquor store.
9. To set up a class in package Equality:
   a) First line must be "package Equality".
   b) Class file must be stored in the Equality Folder.
   c) Any class wanting to use it must import Equality.*;
   d) All of the above.
10. The four principles of OOP are:
    a) Complexity, Polymorphism, Inheritance, Abstraction
    b) Encapsulation, Polymorphism, Inheritance, Abstraction
    c) Encapsulation, Polyandry, Inheritance, Abstraction
    d) Escapism, Polymorphism, Inheritance, Abstraction
    e) Encapsulation, Polymorphism, Inheritance, Absorption

Chapter 10. Encapsulation

Security

There are four levels of security in Java.

Modifier	Class	Package	Children	World
Blank	Yes	Yes	No	No
public	Yes	Yes	Yes	Yes
protected	Yes	Yes	Yes	No
private	Yes	No	No	No

Normally:

- Attributes: private (or at least protected).
- Constant attributes: public
- Methods: public

You set non-constant attributes to private so that only your current class has access to them. Therefore, private is the perfect security level. Occasionally, you might want to allow children to have direct access to your attributes, but this is very rare.

You usually want everyone to be able to access your methods and constants. Therefore, public is used. Rarely, a method only makes sense to a class, so you would use private. I don't see a major reason for a private method.

Modifiers and Accessors

But you might ask, if attributes are private, how do you access them. The answer is through modifiers and accessors. The first thing you define in every class are:

- set methods to set the values for each attribute. (Modifier)
- get methods to get the values for each attribute. (Accessor)

In our current nameAge class, we do not have encapsulation, we have allowed public access to our attributes. This causes two major problems:

- You have lost any ability to restrict access to variables.
- You have lost the ability to apply business rules or conversions to the data.

So, let us put simple modifiers and accessors into our person class and see what it looks like. We will also change our variables to private.

```
public class nameAge{
        private String name;
        private int age;
        public nameAge(){
                name = "";
                age = 0;
        }
        public nameAge(String n, int a){
                this();
                setName(n);
                setAge(a);
        }
        public void setName(String n){
                name = n;
        }
        public void setAge(int a){
                age = a;
        }
        public String getName(){
                return name;
        }
        public int getAge(){
                return age;
        }
        public String toString(){
                String format = "%-20s  %3d";
                String line = String.format(format,name,age);
                return line;
        }
}
```

I modified the driver to use these modifiers. Do
you see the problem?

```
public static void main(String[] args){
        nameAge me = new nameAge("Glen Blood",60);
        System.out.println(me.toString());
        me.setAge(-20);
        me.setName("George Will");
        System.out.println(me.toString());
}
```

Maybe if you see the results:

name = Glen Blood age = 60
name = George Will age = -20

George Will has a negative age. Let's put some
business logic into our setAge method that does not
allow for negative or people older than say 105
years old.

```
public void setAge(int a){
            if ((a >= 0) && (a <= 105))
                    age = a;
}
```

Now this just leaves the age to the previous value so in our case:

name = Glen Blood age = 60
name = George Will age = 60

Which is not perfect but makes more sense than the prior answer.

These accessors and modifiers do not have to be simple. You can use them to change types, change values (for instance modify a birthdate to become an age or combine a first and last name to form a name).

Some other changes in our person class that might make sense:

- Our data comes from a .csv file that contains (name,age). It might make sense to include a constructor that would break out this record and load the object. We can use this to replace the constructor for (name, age).
- We also want to add a setAge method that converts a String input into an age using CSCIConvert.Parse().

So, our person class looks like:

```
public class nameAge{
        private String name;
        private int age;

        public nameAge(){
                name = "";
                age = 0;
        }
        public nameAge(String record){
                this();
                decode(record);
        }
        // accessors
        public String getName(){
                return name;
        }
        public int getAge(){
                return age;
        }
        // mutators
        public void setName(String input){
                name = input;
        }
        public void setAge(int input){
                if ((input >= 0) && (age <= 105))
                        age = input;
        }
        public void setAge(String input){
                int ERROR = 0;
                int number = CSCIConvert.Parse(input,ERROR);
                setAge(number);

        }
        public void decode(String record){
                String[] array;
                array = record.split(",");
                setName(array[0]);
                setAge(array[1]);
        }

        public static String getHeader(){
                String format = "%-20s  %3s";
                String line = String.format(format,"Name","Age");
                return line;
        }

        public String toString(){
                String format = "%-20s  %3d";
                String line = String.format(format,name,age);
                return line;
        }
}
```

Polymorphism

The principle that we are using with our
constructors and setAge is polymorphism. This is
where you have two (or more methods) with the
same name doing the same thing in different ways.
They need to differ in the order or type of the

attributes in the attribute list. Notice we have two constructors

1. age()
2. person(String)

and two setAge methods:

1. setAge(String)
2. setAge(int)

They all do the same respective functions, but in different ways. In fact, the ones with the same name have different parameters.

Review

Encapsulation lets you hide the implementation from the user of your classes. You do that through restricting access to methods through security.

There are several security types, blank, public, private, and protected. The most common are public where anyone can see them and private where only the class see them. Mostly methods are public, and attributes are private.

You can have more than one constructor to allow users to define an object with the initial values without additional code to set those values.

You can use mutators to set/change attributes and accessors to get attributes values.

You can use mutators to force input values to comply to business logic rules such as valid ranges. You can also allow conversions such as String to int or other external data type to internal data type.

You can use accessors to hide the internal data type, to provide computed attributes that are not stored, and get data from external sources.

Questions

1. Accessors:
   a) Get the value of an attribute.
   b) Get the code of a method
   c) Get the security level of a class.
   d) Do nothing.
2. Mutators
   a) Allow you to change the value of an attribute.
   b) Allow you to change the code of a method.
   c) Allow you to change the security level of a class.
   d) Do nothing.
3. Accessors and Mutators can
   a) Be very simpleminded.
   b) Assist in the security of the class.
   c) Hide the implementation of the class.
   d) Hold some of the business logic of the class.
   e) All of the above.
4. Polymorphism allows you to have:
   a) Different names and the same argument lists.
   b) Same name and the same argument list
   c) Same name and different argument lists.
   d) Different names and different argument lists
5. Normally you have
   a) Public attributes and private methods
   b) Private attributes and public methods
   c) Protected attributes and private methods
   d) Protected attributes and public methods
6. Who can access a protected attribute in a class:
   a) Any method in that class
   b) Any method in that class and its children.
   c) Any method in any class.
7. Who can access a public attribute in a class:
   a) Any method in that class
   b) Any method in that class and its children.

c) Any method in any class.
8. Who can access a private attribute in a class:
    a) Any method in that class
    b) Any method in that class and its children.
    c) Any method in any class.
9. If you were distributing your program professionally it is better to:
    a) Distribute your source code with your .class files.
    b) Only distribute your .class files.
    c) Distribute neither.
10. What is the CLASSPATH variable?
    a) A Windows environment variable that tells where classware is found.
    b) A Java compiler environment variable that tells it where to look for packages.
    c) A path to change your social standing.
    d) The direction to this classroom.

Chapter 11. Composition

Composition

One way to reuse classes is through composition. Composition is simply treating a class (or object) as an attribute.

Since String is a class, you used composition the minute you included a String attribute in your class definition.

One difference from a normal primitive variable is that if your attribute class does not have a default constructor, Java cannot execute a default constructor when it instantiates your attribute class. Therefore, you are going to have to build a constructor and instantiate the object with one of its constructors.

Example

Continuing with our idea of building a class to handle our nameage file, why not build an object that holds our entire file. Let's use an ArrayList

```
ArrayList<nameAge> people
```

To hold this ArrayList we will build our class, allages. This goes into another file \GBlood\allAges.java

```
public class allAges{
        private ArrayList<nameAge> people;
        public void allAges(){

        }
}
```

Obviously, we need to fill this out. We need to wrap the normal ArrayList functions like get, add, set, size, and a constructor.

The wrappers are pretty simple and so is our initial constructor.

```
public class allAges{
        private ArrayList<nameAge> people;
        public void allAges(){
                people = new ArrayList<nameAge>();
        }
        public nameAge get(int i){
                int size = people.size();
                if ((i < size) && (i > -1))
                        return people.get(i);
        }
        public void add(nameAge P){
                if (null != P)
                        people.add(P);
        }
        public void set(int i, nameAge P){
                int size = people.size();
                if ((null != P)&& (i < size) && (i > -1))
                        people.set(i,P);
        }
        public int size(){
                return people.size;
        }
}
```

Now do we want to load our ArrayList inside our class or outside of our class. Some people would say, keep the constructors as simple as possible. In this case, I would only be using this class as a conduit to my file. So, let's build a read method. We are going to use a method in our FileIn called readArray that reads in a String array of our csv data and the person constructor to decode it. Remember people is a class variable.

```
public void read(String filename){
        nameAge p;
        String[] records;
        FileIn myFile = new FileIn(filename);
        int size;
        records = myFile.readArray();
        size = records.length;
        for (int i = 0; i < size; ++i){
                p = new nameAge(records[i]);
                people.add(p);
        }
}
```

Now your constructor looks like:

```
public allAges(String filename){
        people = new ArrayList<nameAge>();
        read(filename);
}
```

Get the filename from args[0] and build a driver that spews out the file.

```
public static void main(String[] args){
        String filename = args[0];
        nameAge p;
        allAges records = new allAges(filename);
        int size = records.size();
        for (int i = 0; i < size; ++i){
                p = records.get(i);
                System.out.println(p.toString());
        }
}
```

Now the output from this program works, but it really isn't very pretty.

Marsden	46
Quintessa	7

Vaughan	10
Vivien	84
Nadine	48

The basic object-oriented design model is based on composition. Look at a person. The person has components like a heart, legs, arms, stomach, liver, head, brain. Each of which has other components. The legs have bones radius and ulna, muscles, etc. Some of these components are repeated throughout the body and have attributes and methods of their own.

The first step in object-oriented development is to identify the top- level classes that you need and their attributes and methods. From those attributes, you would identify the component classes. You will start to notice duplications in component classes (or classes that may be share similar attributes and methods).

The next step is to see inheritance patterns, which leads us to our next chapter.

Review

Composition is simply using classes/objects as attributes. You have done this in a simple way every time you added a String to your class.

Our example used an Arraylist of a class that we built in a previous chapter. We then built wrappers for all the supportive methods for the ArrayList and the constructor to load that ArrayList.

Questions

1. Composition is:
    a) The act of writing a paper.
    b) Including other classes/objects as attributes in a class.
    c) Inheriting the attributes and methods of a parent class.
    d) Recycling household trash.
2. Two of the main ways of reuse in OOP are:
    a) Copying code and inheritance.
    b) Composition and inheritance.
    c) Composition and polymorphism.
    d) Encapsulation and inheritance.
3. One reason to use composition is to:
    a) Build a wrapper around a container class.
    b) Reuse the methods from a class.
    c) Instantiate an object of a class.
    d) Fertilize your garden.
4. The keyword for composition is:
    a) compose
    b) add
    c) extends
    d) none of the above.
5. If class xyz has class e (object f) as one of its attributes, and you need to use method e.w() when you instantiate xyz you would:
    a) Just use the method.
    b) Need to write a wrapper for f.w() in class xyz.
    c) Need to write a wrapper for e.w() in class xyz.
    d) Need to copy the source code for the method.
    e) You are out of luck.
6. If class xyz has class e (e does not have a default constructor) (object f) as one of its attributes, the constructor for xyz should:
    a) Execute the constructors for e.

b) Execute the constructors for e if it wants to.
c) The constructor for e is executed automatically when f is declared.
7. (True or False) Composition is rarely used in OOP.
8. (True or False) When you use composition to use a variable your instantiated object gains access to all of its public attributes and methods.
9. The limit on the number of classes/objects you can have as attributes is:
a) 1
b) 2
c) 10
d) No Limit.
10. (True or False) Composition allows me to access protected attributes and methods in a class from a different package.

Chapter 12. Inheritance

Inheritance

Inheritance is the capability of a class to use the attributes and methods of another class without copying them. This is the main way that object-oriented languages reuse software.

Pure object-oriented languages only allow single parent inheritance.

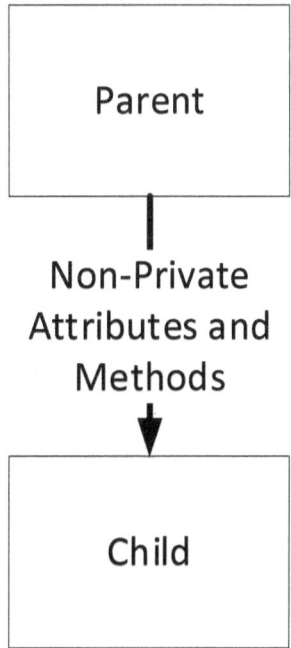

Multiple Inheritance is not allowed

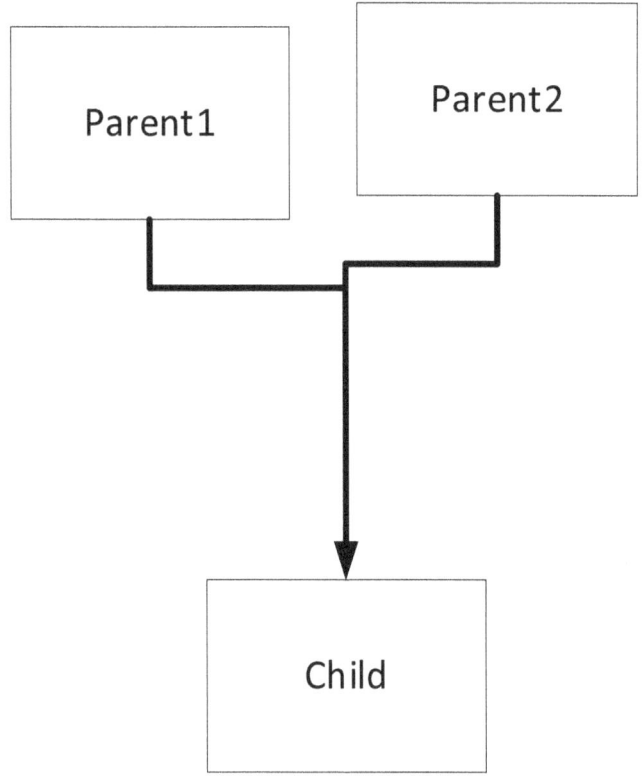

One parent can have multiple children

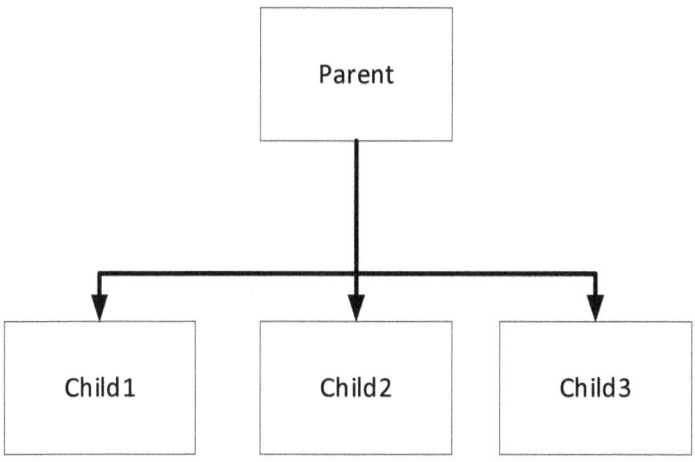

And Children can have children.

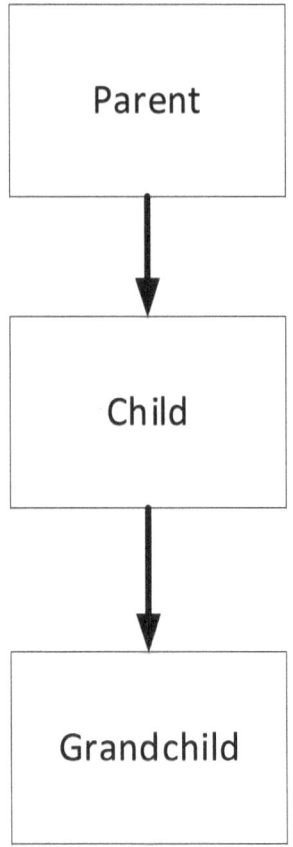

There is no limit as long as the idea of single inheritance is maintained.

Java is a pure object-oriented language. As a matter of fact, on the relational side all objects are descended from a single parent, Object (yes that is the name).

The inheritance keyword is extends. If you want to inherit from a class, you simply type:

```
public class child extends parent{}
```

If your parent is not declared to be final you will be able to use any of its non-private attributes and methods as though you had written them yourself. final is a keyword that says do not allow this class to be a parent. For instance, String is declared to be final.

```
public final class java.lang.String
```

So, you cannot extend String.

Inheritance is used to add attributes and/or methods to a class or modify existing methods without changing the existing class.

Why don't I want to change the existing class? If it is existing, other programs are probably using it. If you change it in any way whatsoever, you might break these programs. Those users will come looking for you. Do not change working code.

Why don't I say subtract attributes or methods? Usually if you are removing things, the inheritance chain is wrong. If you are in the design phase you may be looking at the true parent and not the child.

What happens if I do not need all the attributes or methods from my parent instead of just adding to them? Leave the ones you don't need alone. If you are designing the inheritance hierarchy, you may want to reverse the parent-child relationship.

Constructor

As a basic rule, you need at least one constructor in your child class for each constructor in your parent class. You may not need them all, but it is a good basic rule.

The first line in your constructor should be:

```
super();
```

With the calling parameters that you need.

Add to your constructor the initialization of any new attributes and any activity that you need to have happen.

Attributes

Adding attributes in a child class follow the same rules as in any class. They are usually private to your class and should have public accessor and mutator methods associated with each attribute.

Static attributes have a shared memory location amongst instantiated objects. So, it is rarely a good idea to use them unless they are set to be constant (final static). Even if the information is set once and then kept static, it is still a good idea to keep it private. This way you can prevent your class from having any methods to modify it.

We will discuss shared memory in a later chapter.

Methods

All methods are usually public.

You can override (rewrite) a parent's method by having the same name and calling attributes. For instance: if the parent has a method:

```
move(int);
```

And you declare a method:

```
move(int);
```

With your own implementation in your subclass, your method will be executed for your objects. Unless he declares move to be static or final. Static methods can only be overridden by static methods. Final methods cannot be overridden, you will get a compiler error.

You can also make an additional copy of the method through polymorphism. This is called overloading the method

```
move(String);
```

And there will be two move methods in the child, but one method in the parent.

Remember none of these changes in the child affect the parent in any way.

Example

Looking at our previous file example nameage.csv

We are given a new task to load in a nameageweight.csv file. It has records that look like:

Kelly,40,155
Karen,5,191
Quemby,76,150
Hedda,38,124

We just finished the nameage task and noticed the similarity in the files.

We decided to make a child of nameAge and copy allAges and change the type.

So, our new child nameAgeWeight is basically going to add the weight attribute:

```
private int weight;
```

 add getWeight and setWeight (copies of getAge and setAge)

214

```
public void setWeight(String w){
        int ERROR = -1;
        int weightTest = CSCIConvert.Parse(w,ERROR);
        setWeight(weightTest);
}
public void setWeight(int w){
        if ((w >= 50) && (w <= 900))
                weight = w;
}


public int getWeight(){
        return weight;
}
```

and modify the constructors and the toString
methods.

```
public nameAgeWeight(){
        super();
        weight = 20;
}
public nameAgeWeight(String record){
        this();
        decode(record);
}


public String toString(){
        String format = "%20s  %3d  %6d";
        String line = String.format(format,getName()
                , getAge(), getWeight());
        return line;
}
```

We do not see the variables name or age in our new
class nor can we access them. However, we can
access all the methods from person easily.

We can then copy allAges.java into
allAgeWeights.java and convert nameAge to
nameAgeWeight.

Using our new classes in the driver, the result is:

```
Anthony     34  155
Brett       77  116
Alea         9  163
Darrel      38  190
Nevada       33  132
Kirby       44  169
Mark        70  197
Dane         2  187
Lee         65  122
Ursula       89  129
Ria         27  150
Lucas        59  155
```

So, inheritance, made adding a new attribute easy.
There were minimal code changes. We had
already tested the code in nameAge, so all we
really needed to test was the code associated with
weight.

Other Concerns

You can have a child in the parent's package or in its own if security is maintained. In the latter case, don't forget to import the parent's package.

How do you decide between using inheritance over composition? I would say the decision matrix would be to:

1. Use the class. Name the object to fit your need.
2. Use composition if you need the object to be part of something bigger.
3. Use inheritance if the class has some of what you need, but you need to modify some of the methods or add attributes and/or methods to it.
4. Copy code if you have access to a class' code and you want to need to modify an algorithm.

Review

Composition and inheritance form the basis of reuse in object-oriented programming. They allow you to reuse code without having the source. All you need are the public (or protected) methods interfaces and attributes.

You can only inherit from one parent.

You cannot inherit from a class that has the keyword final in its class header. See String.

The keyword extends allows you to inherit all of the public (or protected) attributes and methods. You can then add your own attributes and methods and override or overload the methods that you inherited.

To override a method, you use the same name and the same calling attribute types (in the same order) as the parent's method.

To overload a method, you use the same name, but change any or all the calling attribute types as the parent's method.

If the parent is in a different package do not forget to import the parent's package.

If you are tempted to remove attributes and/or methods from the parent in your child instead of adding you may have the wrong inheritance chain.

Questions

1. What is the keyword for inheritance?
   a) child of
   b) uses
   c) extends
   d) inherits
2. An overloaded method has the _ as its parent method.
   a) Same name and same calling attributes.
   b) Same name and different calling attributes.
   c) Different name and same calling attributes.
   d) Different name and different calling attributes.
3. An overridden method has the _ as its parent method.
   a) Same name and same calling attributes.
   b) Same name and different calling attributes.
   c) Different name and same calling attributes.
   d) Different name and different calling attributes.
4. The main OOP reuse methods do not include:
   a) Inheritance.
   b) Method libraries.
   c) Composition.
   d) Class libraries.
5. (True of False) A child class can access a private attribute directly.
6. (True or False) A child class in a different package must use the import statement to inherit from the parent.
7. What keyword keeps a class from being a parent:
   a) final
   b) static
   c) closed
   d) All classes can be parents.

8. If I need two classes. Class A has two methods. Class B has those same two methods and a third method. What should the inheritance pattern be?
    a) A should be the parent of B.
    b) A should be the child of B.
    c) No inheritance pattern exists.
9. One reason to make attributes public is to:
    a) Enable shared variables.
    b) Enable shared constants.
    c) There is never any reason to make attributes public.
10. You can inherit from at most _ parent(s).
    a) 1
    b) 2
    c) 4
    d) As many as you want.

Chapter 13. Abstraction

Abstraction

In java, abstraction is the idea that you can write a class or method that can be defined without a body, so that you can declare its implementation later through inheritance.

An abstract method is a method whose header is defined but does not have a body.

For example: Let us say you wanted a generic method that gave you the area from an object.

```
public abstract double area();
```

An abstract class is a class that contains abstract methods. It may include non-abstract methods. It may include data. But, it must have at least one abstract method:

```
public abstract class shape{

        public abstract double area();
}
```

Suppose we wanted to expand this idea to have a set of shapes, such as circles, squares, and rectangles. And be able to declare their areas and circumferences we might want to start with a generic shape.

Abstract shape:

```
public abstract class shape{

        public abstract double area();
        public abstract double circumference();

        public String toString(){
                String line = "Area = " + area()
                + " Circumference = " + circumference();
                return line;
        }
}
```

Circle

```
public class circle extends shape{
        private double radius;
        public circle(){
                super();
        }
        public circle(double r){
        super();
        setRadius(r);
        }
        public circle(String s){
                super();
                setRadius(s);
        }
        public void setRadius(double r){
                if (r > 0) radius = r;
        }
        public void setRadius(String s){
                double ERROR = 0;
                double r = CSCIConvert.Parse(s,ERROR);
                setRadius(r);
        }
        public double getRadius(){
                return radius;
        }
        public double area(){
                return Math.PI * radius * radius;
        }
        public double circumference(){
                return Math.PI * 2 * radius;
        }
        public String toString(){
                String line;
                line = "Circle radius = " + getRadius()
                + " " + super.toString();
                return line;
        }
}
```

Square

```
public class square extends shape{
        private double side;
        public square(){
                super();
        }
        public square(double s1){
                super();
                setSide(s1);
        }
        public square(String s1){
                super();
                setSide(s1);
        }
        public void setSide(double r){
                if (r > 0) side = r;
        }
        public void setSide(String s){
                double ERROR = 0;
                double r = CSCIConvert.Parse(s,ERROR);
                setSide(r);
        }
        public double getSide(){
                return side;
        }
        public double area(){
                return side * side;
        }
        public double circumference(){
                return 4 * side;
        }
        public String toString(){
                String line;
                line = "Square sides = " + getSide()
                + " " + super.toString();
                return line;
        }
}
```

Rectangle

```
public class rectangle extends shape{
        private double side1;
        private double side2;

        public rectangle(){
                super();
        }
        public rectangle(double s1, double s2){
                super();
                setSide1(s1);
                setSide2(s2);
        }
        public rectangle(String s1, String s2){
                super();
                setSide1(s1);
                setSide2(s2);
        }
        public void setSide1(double r){
                if (r > 0) side1 = r;
        }
        public void setSide1(String s){
                double ERROR = 0;
                double r = CSCIConvert.Parse(s,ERROR);
                setSide1(r);
        }
        public double getSide1(){
                return side1;
        }
        public void setSide2(double r){
                if (r > 0) side2 = r;
        }
        public void setSide2(String s){
                double ERROR = 0;
                double r = CSCIConvert.Parse(s,ERROR);
                setSide2(r);
        }
        public double getSide2(){
                return side2;
        }
        public double area(){
                return side1 * side2;
        }
        public double circumference(){
                return 2 * side1 + 2 * side2;
        }
        public String toString(){
                String line;
                line = "Rectangle sides = " + getSide1()
                + " x " + getSide2()
                        + " " + super.toString();
                return line;
        }
}
```

So, a Driver program looks like:

```
public static void main(String[] args){
        // get two sides from the command line.
        String side1 = args[0];
        String side2 = args[1];
        // build two circles, one using a
        // constructor and the other
        // using its mutator.
        circle circlea = new circle(side1);
        circle circleb = new circle();
        circleb.setRadius(side2);
        // build a rectangle.
        rectangle rect = new rectangle(side1,side2);
        // build two squares, one using a constructor
        // and the other
        // using its mutator.

        square sq1 = new square(side1);
        square sq2 = new square();
        sq2.setSide(side2);
        // print out the shapes to standard out
        System.out.println(circlea.toString());
        System.out.println(circleb.toString());
        System.out.println(rect.toString());
        System.out.println(sq1.toString());
        System.out.println(sq2.toString());
}
```

A second Example

Is it possible to write an abstract class for the file problem that we saw in nameAge and nameAgeWeight. I hope that you will notice code that could be shared for any CSV file.
If you do a javap on nameAge you can see the public methods.

```
public class GBlood.nameAge {
  public GBlood.nameAge();
  public GBlood.nameAge(java.lang.String);
  public java.lang.String getName();
  public int getAge();
  public void setName(java.lang.String);
  public void setAge(int);
  public void setAge(java.lang.String);
  public void decode(java.lang.String);
  public static java.lang.String getHeader();
  public java.lang.String toString();
}
```

Our abstract class call it abstractPerson would want
to have two constructors and an abstract toString.

```
public abstractPerson(){}
public abstractPerson(String record){
        this();
        list = splitter(record);
}
    public abstract String toString();
```

And a non-abstract splitter method.

```
public String[] splitter(String record){
        String[] list;
        list = record.split(",");
        return list;
}
```

The fun begins when we look at our ArrayList
Class.

The key is that the ArrrayList is capable of holding
data for any child of abstractRecord

```
private ArrayList<abstractPerson> people;
```

You might have a problem with this shared
variable if you had two files with the same format
that you were loading using the same subclass.
Otherwise I don't see a problem.

It has the same wrappers as in our previous
ArrayList cases. The only one that needs to be
overridden is get. To change the return type.
Return types are not noticed by the compiler in
polymorphism.

```
/**  Override get to modify the output to your class */
public abstractPerson get(int i){
        int size = people.size();
        if ((i < size) && (i > -1))
                return people.get(i);
        return null;
}
```

In order to use the read method, you must override the abstract instantiate method to instantiate your child:

```
public abstract abstractPerson instaniate(String record).
/** must be instantiated by child */
/** new abstractPerson(record); */
```

So, after you write a record that looks like the nameAge class from the previous chapter as a child of abstractRecord, your file class is built by writing one short constructor and overriding two short methods.

```
public bodyFile(String filename){
        super(filename);
}

public body get(int i){

        body me = (body) super.get(i);
        return me;
}
public body instaniate(String record){
        body me = new body(record);
        return me;
}
```

And a subset of the results are:

Luke	38
Venus	63
Selma	78
Kelly	9
Alyssa	67
Clarke	57
Thane	70
Cameron	25
Julie	65

Review

Abstraction is the concept of an ultimate parent. One that is a pure template for its children. It has no way to exist on its own. You cannot instantiate it.

An abstract class is defined as a class that has one or more abstract methods. It has the keyword abstract in its class header.

An abstract method is defined as a method that has no body. It has the keyword abstract in its method header.

You will very rarely build abstract classes, but you will need to know about them.

You may not realize that an abstract class is useful or needed until after you build a few non-abstract classes with very similar functionality.

Unfortunately, the only way to test abstract classes, is to build a simple non-abstract child and test that child.

Questions

1. An abstract class is:
   a) A class that cannot be instantiated.
   b) A blueprint class for other classes.
   c) A class that has at least on abstract method.
   d) All of the above.
2. An abstract method:
   a) Has no body.
   b) Has no calling parameters.
   c) Has no return value.
   d) None of the above.
3. (True or False) An abstract class cannot have any attributes.
4. To inherit from an abstract class, you must:
   a) Override all the abstract methods.
   b) Overload all the abstract methods.
   c) Override some of the abstract methods.
   d) Overload some of the abstract methods.
5. (True or False) You can use the keyword final in an abstract class' header.
6. (True or False) You should always build an abstract class.
7. (True or False) When you build an abstract class the child classes are always smaller than the parent class.
8. Abstract classes are ways to:
   a) Build templates for groups of classes.
   b) Simplify the creation of classes.
   c) Store constants.
   d) All of the above.
9. (True or False) You will always know that you need an abstract class when you first look at a problem.
10. (True or False) Abstract classes serve no useful purpose in Java.

Chapter 14. Interface

Interface

One use of abstract classes is to create an interface.
An interface is a method java uses to break the
single parent rule of inheritance.

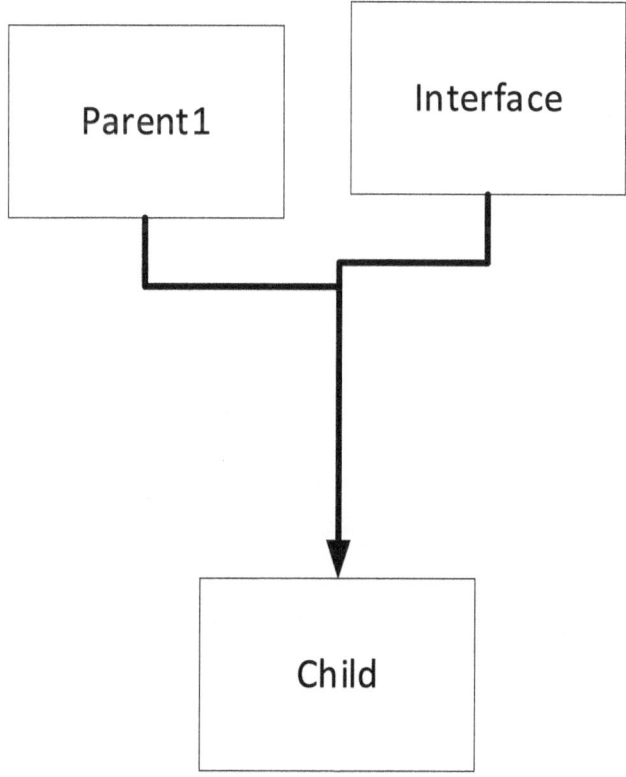

There is no real limit on the number of interfaces that one uses, however you need to be reasonable. Like everything else consider maintainability and understandability.

Interfaces consist of abstract classes with only abstract and static methods and constant (static final) variables.

What is an interface good for?

Interfaces allow you to inherit method definitions.

For instance, one of the interfaces that we will use immediately is the Comparator. Comparator is in java.util. The comparator allows us to use sorts in arrays and ArrayLists for objects.

In order to implement the Comparator interface properly, I had to build some simple sorting classes.

```
public class abstractSort implements Comparator<abstractRecord>{

        public  int compare(abstractRecord a, abstractRecord b){
                return 0;
        }
}
```

And its child

```
public class bodySort extends abstractSort{
public int compare(abstractRecord a, abstractRecord b){
                    // comparable method


            // This object T must be an instance of the same class.
            // returns -1, 0 or 1
            if (!(a instanceof body)) return -1;
            if (!(b instanceof body)) return -1;

            body first = (body) a;
            body second = (body) b;

            // get the differences in age and name
            int ageDiff = first.getAge() - second.getAge();
            int nameDiff = first.getName().compareToIgnoreCase(second.getName());

            // Sort by age.  If the age is the same sort by name.
            if (0 == ageDiff){
                    return nameDiff;
            }

            return ageDiff;
    }

}
```

So, in abstractFile, I needed to implement the sort method. abstractFile was the only class that had direct access to people. I also built a method getMethod that allowed me to have the children send their sort methods to the sort.

```
public  void sort(){
        Collections.sort(people, getSortMethod());
}

// override This method to sort properly
public abstractSort getSortMethod(){
        abstractSort sorter = new abstractSort();
        return sorter;
}
```

So in bodyFile we needed to implement
getSortMethod()

```
// override This method to sort properly
        public bodySort getSortMethod(){
        bodySort sorter = new bodySort();
        return sorter;
    }
```

And in bodyDriver we add in the command

```
records.sort();
```

And our output looks like:

Amery	1
Julie	3
Adria	4
Elliott	4
Germane	5
Jena	7

This is sorted by age and then by name, to sort by name and then by age, we could write a different sort class.

Collisions

Unlike inheritance, multiple interfaces can be used at the same time. What happens if they define the same attribute or method? This is called a collision. The compiler does not solve collisions. You must explicitly resolve them. So, if you have two interfaces (a and b) with the same attribute (q) and you say implements a, b. The compiler would not accept q. It would accept a.q or b.q.

Review

The interface is the method that Java uses to get around the one parent inheritance rule.

It avoids some of the issues of multiple inheritance in two ways. Interfaces must be abstract classes with only abstract and static methods and constant (static final) attributes.

The keyword implements allows you to access the interface.

To avoid collisions, you must explicitly resolve them.

Questions

1. How many interfaces can a class use:
    a) 1
    b) 2
    c) 4
    d) As many as you need.
2. An interface must be an abstract class without:
    a) Abstract methods.
    b) Constant attributes.
    c) Non-abstract methods.
    d) All of the above.
3. The interface header differs from an abstract class header.
    a) They are the same, abstract class.
    b) The key word interface instead of abstract class
    c) The keyword interface instead of abstract
    d) The keyword interface instead of class.
4. The keyword to use an interface is:
    a) interfaces with
    b) extends
    c) implements
    d) uses
5. Collisions (two interfaces with the same attribute or method) are handled by:
    a) Random chance
    b) First interface listed is selected.
    c) Programmer must explicitly choose.
    d) Last interface listed is selected.
6. (True or False) You must implement all methods in an interface.
7. (True or False) Interfaces are the best way to share constant attributes.
8. (True or False) Interfaces are better than inheritance since they allow you to break the single parent rule.

9. (True or False) Interfaces are a way to enforce API standards.
10. (True or False) all attributes in an interface are final static.

Chapter 15. Parallel Processing

Have you ever wanted to duplicate yourself so that you can do two things at once? Well you still can't do that, but your computer can.

Architectures

There are several ways for computers to be built to enable parallel processing.

Multiple computers linked together

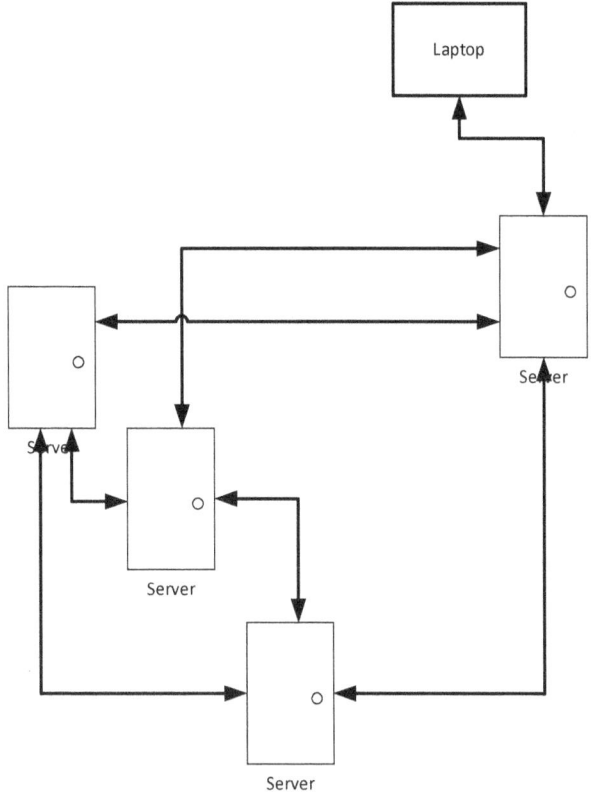

Teradata database systems did this very effectively starting in the 1980's. Teradata uses a shared nothing architecture to allow extremely large databases with great response time. These systems are separate computers bound with a proprietary high bandwidth connection. They use a pretty generic SQL to access their database. Their two largest customers are AT&T and Walmart.

Multiple processors.

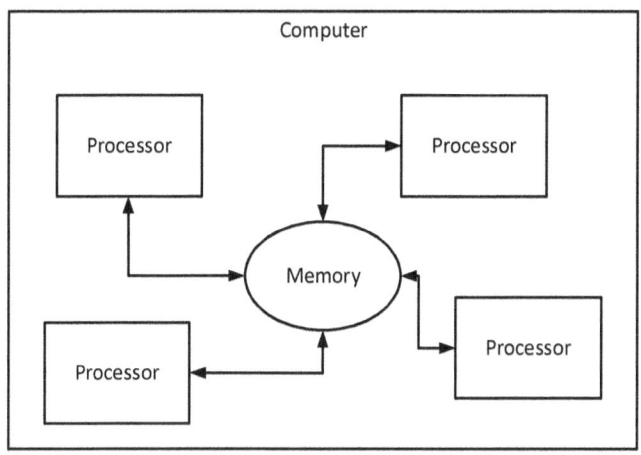

In these systems, hardware and software were designed from the ground up to be multiprocessor systems. Some examples were Cray computers and They required specialized programming to make effective use of the multiple processors.

Cray computers were used for years to make weather forecast predictions at Air Force Global Weather Central.

The growth in multiple processor computers has also led to a renewed interest in functional (aka recursive) languages, such as Lisp.

Multiple cores.

A similar architecture to multiple processor is multiple cores. Multiple cores are multiple CPUs on the same chip. Therefore, they will share the same memory.

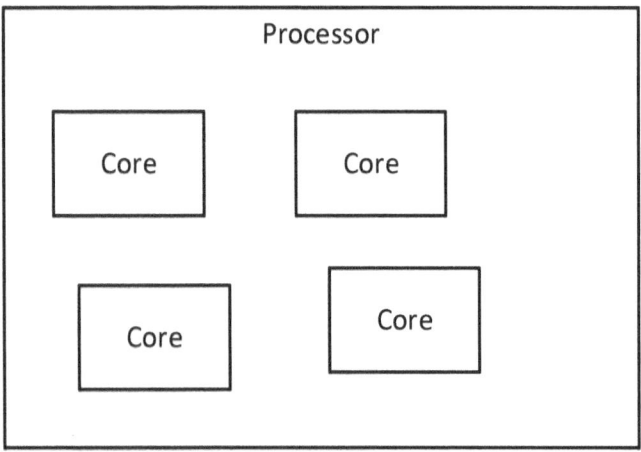

Hyper-Threading

Hyper-Threading is like multiple cores, however instead of a hardware solution, it is a software solution.

Single Processor

Yes, even single processors allowed mutiltasking. They usually allowed multiple processes or programs to run at one time. They were several methods used to accomplish this. The most successful, and I believe the one that is used by most (if not all) operating system today is the concept of a time slice.

Alpha	Bravo	Charlie	Alpha	Bravo	Charlie	Alpha	Bravo	Charlie
Time ->								

Some short (to a human) time period is separated into time slices. Processes are then allowed to run

246

for a slice of time and then placed in a queue (priority or non-priority) to wait their turn to run again. These time slices are so small that unless you have a lot of processes running, you don't notice any significant delay.

If a process is waiting on I/O or something else, it is placed in a heap and not on the queue until its wait is over.

Threads

What happens to a process when it is waiting for processor time? Each active process has information in registers in the CPU that tell the processor what memory it is using, what command it is on, and other information about the process. This is called the current processor state. That state is placed on a heap. The operating system time sharing process keeps track of each process and the heap address of its state. So, when process A's turn is over and process B's turn comes up, and process A's state is downloaded to the heap and process B's state is loaded into the registers. This takes time. This is referred to as overhead.

The larger the processes state is, the larger the overhead. So, they came up with the ideas of threads.

There are two types Heavyweight Threads and Lightweight Threads.

Heavyweight Threads are usually individual processes with their own address space. So, they will have a large state and a large overhead. They can be spawned by processes or by the operating system. Your program is a heavyweight thread.

Lightweight Threads have smaller states than processes. They do not live by themselves. They do not have their own address space. They are spawned by processes and some of their identify and state is controlled by the parent process. Since their state is much smaller than heavyweight processes, their overhead is much lower.

To effectively handle multitasking, it takes a large memory and a fast processor.

Java Multitasking

Java uses lightweight threads to perform multitasking. They use the runnable interface to define threads with the method run().

Like everything else in java there are several choices. The best one seems to be to extend the Thread class.

```
public class java.lang.Thread implements java.lang.Runnable
```

You create your thread in the class constructor.

You must override the method run(). This is your actual thread activity.

```
public void run();
```

A simple program, testThreads, just runs two threads that writes out a message 30 times. If you run this, you end up with a combination of First and Seconds. You can try changing the Priority and see what happens.

Thread class

```
public class Writer extends Thread {
  // shared memory
          private int counter = 1;
          String message;
  public Writer(String message ) {
    this.message = message;
  }
    public void run( ) {
      while (counter < 30 ){
          System.out.println( message + " @ " + counter);
          ++counter;

    }
  }
}
```

Driver TestThreads

```
public static void main( String args [] ) {

        Thread first = new Writer("First");
        first.setPriority( Thread.NORM_PRIORITY);
        Thread second = new ShowThread("Second");
        second.setPriority( Thread.NORM_PRIORITY);
        first.start();
        second.start();
}
```

start() is the built in method that starts the thread.

Shared Nothing

Now this does not seem very intuitive, but as you can see, each thread is independent. They do not share information or memory space between each other. This is called **shared nothing**. There are useful problems that can be solved using this memory model.

A problem that we have seen before (Chapter 8) that is designed for this solution is the Fibonacci recursive solution. If you will recall, the problem with the recursive solution is that the process breaks up into different processes that need to recalculate the same solution. Assuming that you have enough processors, you can cause the separate processes to run on separate processors in unison and get the solution that way.

The recursive method was

```
public static double RecursiveFactorial(int n){
if (n <= 1) return 1;
return n * RecursiveFactorial(n - 1);
} // end RecursiveFactorial
```

So, each RecursiveFibonacci becomes a thread.

There are two internal attributes

```
private int value;
private double finalValue;
```

The constructor sets the initial value (n)

```
public fibonacci(int value ) {
  this.value = value;
  }
```

The run method is the recursive method, you can break it up into a few pieces

The return from recursion

```
if (value <= 1) {
        // System.out.println("Fib + " + value);
        finalValue = value;
}
```

The actual recursive threads

```
fibonacci fibm1 = new fibonacci(value -1);
fibonacci fibm2 = new fibonacci(value -2);

fibm1.start();
fibm2.start();
```

And the return from the threads. We do need to wait for each thread to complete, so we use the method join().

```
try{
        fibm1.join();
fibm2.join();
}
catch(InterruptedException e){
        System.out.println("*** Execution was inte
}
finalValue = fibm1.getValue() + fibm2.getValue();
```

And we use the method getValue() to get the solution to fibonacci(value-1) + Fibonacci(value-2).

```
// this method allows us to return the value to
// external processses without sharing memory.
public double getValue(){
        return finalValue;
}
```

Using a method or API to share information between classes is referred to as messaging. So our main method starts the first thread and waits for all of the threads to complete. Note, there is more code to set up time counters, but this is the most critical code.

You start the initial thread

```
fibonacci fib = new fibonacci(value);

fib.setPriority( Thread.NORM_PRIORITY);
```

And then you use the join command to get all threads to complete.

```
try{
        fib.join();
}
catch(InterruptedException e){
        System.out.println("*** Execu
}
```

Much like the program in chapter 8, it takes the value from the command line and if greater than 2, it starts a fibonacci thread and when finished displays the solution and time spent.

On my I7 Single processor (6 core) machine, a seed value of 6 or 8 the time differences were not bad 1-2 milliseconds from the iterative and recursive and 4 to 8 milliseconds for the thread method. By 20, it was obvious. 0 -2 milliseconds for iterative and recursive, and 2,763 milliseconds for thread. Now with more real processors, I would expect better results for the thread method.

The question comes up, does Java use the multiple processors available. First, the literature states that it does. Second, through Resource Monitor, I observed greatly increased activity on all cores during the process activity.

So why would the thread recursive method take so much more time than the non-thread recursive method? Each time a thread is started, there is overhead of generating a small state (a register and memory definition) for that thread. Each time that thread is moved out of the active state into the inactive state (and vice-versa) takes time. Since by the time we get to 20, there are more processes running than there are logical or physical CPU's we have threads swapping in and out of CPU space. This overhead probably accounts for the additional time.

So, are thread processes worthless on a non-multiple processor system? No. They are useful for asynchronous programs such as graphical user interface (GUI) programs. They may be useful for communications between asynchronous programs. You may find other uses for them.

We have looked at shared-nothing programs. How do we share information between threads? There are several methods.

Messaging

A simple way to share information between processes without sharing memory is messaging. This is usually accomplished by using the class methods of a different thread. We saw this in the Fibonnaci problem when we used the getValue() method.

Shared Memory Models

We will use a bank problem to discuss some of the problems with sharing memory.

Our bank model will consist of two basic classes:

> bankAccount – The account (account number and balance)
> bankAction - The action deposit or withdrawal (account number, action, status)

And two collection classes:

> accountList – Through composition, will hold an array of unique bankAccount sorted by accountNumber.

> actionList – Through composition, will hold an ArrayList of bankAction sorted by action.

The threads will be held in the class, takeAction which will be spun off by the main in bank.

254

```
accountList accounts = new accountList(bankFilename);
actionList actions = new actionList(actionFilename);
// build the independent action thread objects.
takeAction one = new takeAction(accounts, actions);
takeAction two = new takeAction(accounts, actions);
takeAction three = new takeAction(accounts, actions);

// start alll of the independent action threads.
// we are going to run three.  We could add more.
one.start();
two.start();
three.start();
```

Shared Read only Memory

The simplest model would be to share a common
read-only memory bank. Such as a set of
constants. This should be declared final in order to
avoid inadvertent modification to that memory
bank by one process (or several).

Each thread (takeAction) will share the memory
address of:

```
public static accountList accounts;
public static actionList actions;
```

We can share this memory, because these two
addresses are fixed.

Shared Writable Memory

The second model is shared memory that can be
modified. The trick here is to avoid having
processes overwriting each other. That is having
one process modifying the value while another is
reading it or planning to write it.

Segmented Memory

You could define different sets of that memory to different processes, for example different parts of an array, but that is not sharing the memory location. You could call this separate access for each process.

In our bank Problem, we have the actionList. Each action is taken one time and one time only. Under common bank rules, all deposits must be applied before withdrawals, therefore, we sort the actions by action ("D" before "W"). We use sharedCounter count (which uses a simple lock to control access):

```
public sharedCounter(int start){
        counter = start;
}
public int incCounter(){
        l.lock();
                ++counter;
        l.unlock();
        return counter;
}
```

Starting from 0 (by initialize at -1) to traverse the actionlist and get an action until the end of the list (size is the number of records in actionList).

```
int c = count.incCounter();
// keep working while there are actions to perform.
while (c < size){
        // get the action
        myAction = actions.get(c);
        // Act on the account
        accounts.act(myAction);
        // set the status
        actions.set(c,myAction);
        // get the next one to work on
        // Note:  not sequential another thread
        // might get the intervening action
        c = count.incCounter();
}
```

Each time through the loop, you always get the
next available action because c is the next
incremented integer and is thread safe. So, we
never have two concurrent processes accessing the
same bankAction or ActionList item. We do not
need to lock either the bankAction or ActionList.
You can use this logic anytime you use segmented
memory.

Lockable Memory

The other memory model we use requires the read
and write locks.

Bank Transactions

A classic problem in multiprocessing is the bank
account transaction problem. A bank account has
two basic types of transactions, deposits and
withdrawals. The bank account consists of an
account number and a balance (say $20.00). Now

suppose you have two processes (a and b) accessing the same account:

Process a is a withdrawal of $5.00
Process b is a deposit of $10.00

So, if both processes ran sequentially, you would have an end balance of (20 – 5 + 10) $25.00

Process a reads the balance of $20.00
Process b reads the balance of $20.00
Process a subtracts $5.00 to have a balance of $15.00
Process b adds $10.00 to have a balance of $30.00.
Process a stores the balance of $15.00
Process b stores the balance of $30.00

Of course, with multiple threads there is no way to predict the outcome, so the balance could be $15.00, $20.00, or $30.00. We all know (and hope) that banks do not work this way. So, we introduce the concept of locks.

The basic concept of a lock is that once invoked no other process is allowed to enter a set of code until the lock is released. All other processes are left in a queue to wait, until the lock is released. Then the next process is allowed to grab the lock.

There are three basic types of clean locks:

A straightforward lock.

Only one process is allowed to have this lock at a time.

258

A write lock

> Only one process is allowed to have this lock at a time. Processing starts when all relating read locks are cleared.

A read lock

> A process that requests this lock is allowed to have this lock as long as the related write lock is not active. Processing starts immediately. If a write lock is active, then processes wait to get the read lock until the write lock is released.

The basic lock code looks like:

```
l.lock;
    code
l.unlock;
```

The java lock package is
java.util.concurrent.locks.;

 We chose arrays for accountList so that we don't have to lock the accountList while we get the bankAccount object and then set it. By using arrays, we can act on it directly. So that the relevant line of code in accountList.act(bankAction action) is

```
// act on that account.  set completion or failure.
success = accounts[pos].act(action,amount);
```

And bankAccount.act(char action, int amount)

```
// act on the account
public boolean act (char action, int amount){
        boolean success = false;
        // action has been tested earlier it is either D or W.
        if ('D' == action) {
                success = deposit(amount);

        }
        else { // ('W' == action)
                success = withdraw(amount);
        }
        return success;
}
```

Locks

To see how the write locks work, look at deposit
(withdrawal is almost identical)

```
wAccount.lock();
        actual = amount ; // make amount = pennies
        if (actual >  0){
                balance = balance + actual;
            success = true;
        }
        else{
                System.out.println(
                "Must deposit positive amounts");
            success = false;
        }
wAccount.unlock();
```

You will see that we are locking the minimal
amount of code. We do not want to retain the
locks very long, since we do not want to cause
other processes to have to wait.

To see the read lock in action, look at
bankAccount.getBalance()

```
rAccount.lock();
        tempBalance = balance;
rAccount.unlock();
```

The accountNumber does not need a lock since it never changes.
The entire code will be available on the flash-drive in javabook/chpt15 .

Thread Program (Revisited)

A smaller program that combines our first program with sharedCounter.

The thread program is changed to use sharedCounter in the run() method

```
public void run( ) {
        int counter = c.incCounter();
        while (counter <= 10 ){
                System.out.println( message
                + " @ " + counter);
                counter = c.incCounter();

        }
}
```


Because of the wait queues it forces an order on the threads that we did not see before:

First @ 1
Second @ 2
First @ 3
Second @ 4
First @ 5
Second @ 6

Pipes

A different method of communication between processes is using pipes aka message queues. This is very similar to flat files; except they are in memory and active.

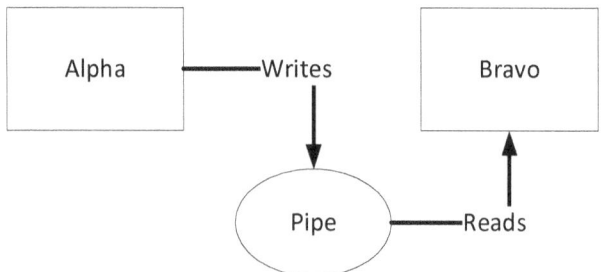

Pipes are one direct or unidirectional. This means that information can travel only one way along them. You must use two pipes for two-way communication.

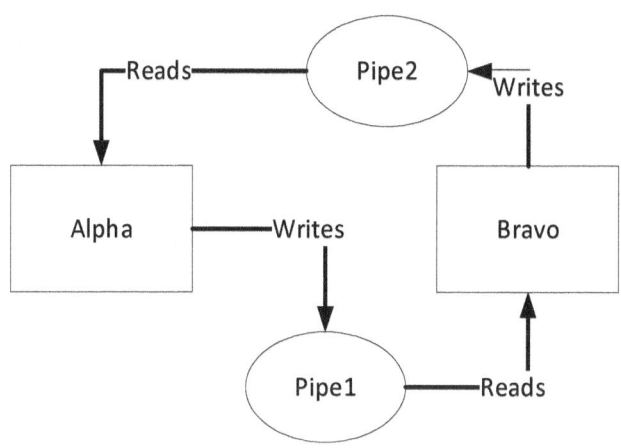

Pipes use system memory and not the file system, so they are much faster than using files. They are set up so that bytes travel along them. (remember Unicode takes two bytes). I built a class commPipe (in CSCI) that would let you read or send a String via a pipe. It defines a pair of connected pipes (input and output). You can then use this class to build two processes to communicate via these pipes.

I then built a program that would read in a file and write it standard output using two processes.

```
public static void main(String args[] ) {
        // get the input file from the command line.
        String inputFile = args[0];
        // define the pipes.
        commPipe pipes = new commPipe();
        // define the file reader
        fileReadSend reader = new fileReadSend(pipes,inputFile);
        // define the writer.
        pipeSpew writer = new pipeSpew(pipes);

        // start the two processes.  When the reader
        // ends so will the writer.
        reader.start();
        writer.start();

}
```

There are many other things that you can do using pipes, such as reversing the data. I believe that this is most useful when shared memory is not available (separate machines).

This process reads the file and sends each line to the pipe.

```
// thread process
    public void run(){
            String line;
            // primer read
            line = myFile.Read();
            while (null != line){
                    // send the line down the pipe
                    pipes.write(line);
                    // read the next line
                    line = myFile.Read();
            }
            // close the file and the pipe
            myFile.close();
            pipes.close();
    }
```

This process takes a line of data off the pipe and spews it to standard output.

```
        }
        // thread process
        public void run(){
                // primer read
                String line = pipes.read();
                while(null != line){
                        /// send output to stadard out.
                        System.out.println(line);
                        // get next line
                        line = pipes.read();
                }
                // close pipe
                pipes.closeIn();
        }
```

Note: commPipe hides a lot of the complexity of setting up a pipe pair. To set up two-way communication you would need two commPipes. This does not have to be used for files. It could be used for any String.

Review

Multiprocessing is a powerful but dangerous tool. Producing thread safe processes requires careful design.

To produce threads one needs to extend Thread and have a method run().

Then the calling routine has to start() each thread.

To bring them together when they finish one uses the join() method which must be enclosed in a try{}catch(InterruptedException e){} block.

There are many memory models for threads:
- Shared nothing. All information is passed when the thread is opened and passed back when it is closed.
- Shared memory
  a) Static memory.
  b) Segmented memory.
  c) Using locks (lock, read and write lock) to keep processes from writing over each other.

Pipes. Communicating over an asynchronous path.

One thing to be careful of is to avoid generating too many threads and overwhelming your system. I believe that this is what we saw in the Fibonacci problem.

Questions

1. The main parallel processing models do not include:
    a) Multi-processors
    b) Multi-core
    c) Hyper-threading
    d) Hyper-warp
2. To achieve artificial parallel processing in a single processor architecture, most systems today use:
    a) Time-slicing.
    b) Cooperative multitasking.
    c) Bribery.
    d) None of the above.
3. The biggest risk in the parallel processing shared memory model is:
    a) None.
    b) Two processes reading the same memory at the same time.
    c) Two processes writing to the same memory at the same time.
4. Memory Locks are used to ensure:
    a) That processes run slowly.
    b) That no process reads from a memory location that is about to be written to.
    c) That no two processes read from the same memory location at the same time.
    d) To make code more complicated.
5. Pipes are:
    a) Faster than files.
    b) Slower than files.
    c) Impossible to tell.

6. The basic shared memory models include all but:
   a) Read only memory
   b) Memory Locks
   c) Pipes
   d) Segmented memory
7. The parallel processing method is:
   a) run()
   b) start()
   c) parallel()
   d) methodname() executes runnable{}
8. If you have more than one thread running and you want to get the results when they finish you use the _ method.
   a) start()
   b) stop()
   c) end()
   d) join()
9. To basic unit of a parallel process is called the:
   a) Runnable
   b) Process
   c) Thread
   d) Program
10. A thread's state includes:
   a) All attributes current values.
   b) Current program execution step.
   c) The execution heap.
   d) All of the above.

Chapter 16. Graphical User Interfaces

Simple and Complex Graphical user Interfaces (GUI)s can be written in in Java.

Simple GUIs

Simple GUIs are easy using the JOptionPane class's static methods. For instance, an easy Hello world program, like we wrote in chapter two, which produces a nice box like:

Takes only one import statement and JOptionPane's showMessageDialog() method.

```
JOptionPane.showMessageDialog( null
, "Hello World!" );
```

The class JoptionPane does all of the work. We can also have a simple question/answer program using showInputDialog():

Using the showInputDialog() method.

```
String name =
JOptionPane.showInputDialog( null
, "Please tell me your name" );
JOptionPane.showMessageDialog(null
, "Hello " + name);
```

Using showOptionDialog, you can get answers to simple questions.

If I hit Yes

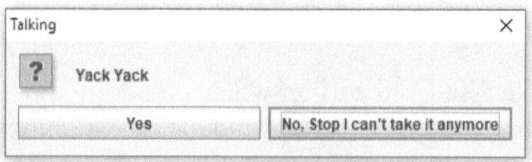

If I hit Yes a couple of more times.

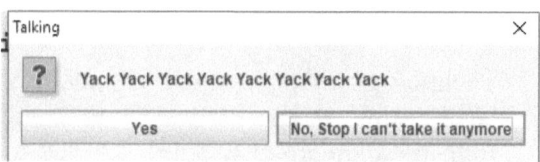

So, finally I hit "No, Stop I can't take it anymore" and it exits.

```
boolean continueLoop = true;
String message = "Yack ";
int choice;
Object[] options = {"Yes",
"No, Stop I can't take it anymore"};
while (continueLoop){
        choice = JOptionPane.showOptionDialog(null
        , message,"Talking"
        ,JOptionPane.YES_NO_OPTION,
        JOptionPane.QUESTION_MESSAGE
        ,null,options,options[1]);
        message = message + message;
        continueLoop = (choice < 1);
}
```

Of course, you usually want more complex GUIs and Java provides classes to assist you with those tasks.

GUI Design

As we discussed earlier, when we design any program, we want to separate the business logic from the input/output logic. This is an order of magnitude more important for GUIs. Quite often, GUI requirements will change (often during development) due to:

> Technology changes in the front end.
> User desires and aesthetics.
> Industry standard changes.

So how is this accomplished. One method is by developing the multi-tier approach, using asynchronous processes. This can be accomplished through software, hardware or a mixture of both. It looks like:

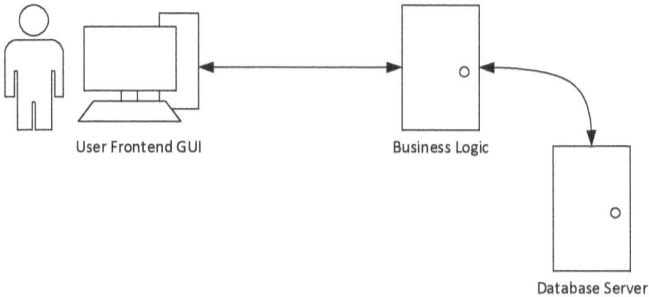

Or with an internet-based application

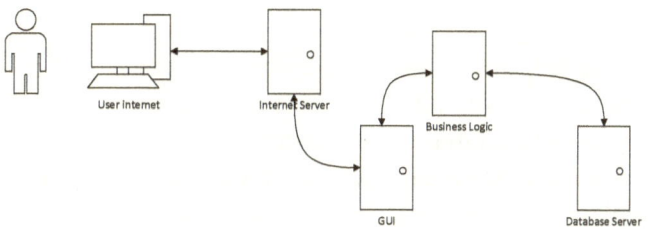

Since, the business logic and the GUI are asynchronous and separate processes, you can see that the discussions about multiprocessing and communication become important.

We will not discuss internet-based GUIs or databases in this course. You will have other courses for these topics. So, our logical model is:

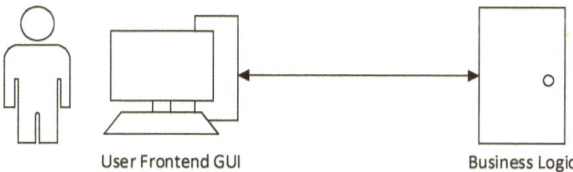

And physically everything will be on the same system.

A word of warning. Your programs will involve a ton of similar objects. Be very careful in how you name them. Java has all the tools you need to build extremely cool and complex GUIS and graphical programs. However, I have major concerns with using Java for this purpose:

The number of objects and level of detail required may make the final code unmaintainable unless we are extremely dedicated in keeping good design standards.

The tedium of building objects may cause us to skip steps and take shortcuts that harm the final product and make it unmaintainable.

The lack of visual graphical tools makes object placement tough and will lead to multiple trial runs, especially when working with customers. This reminds me of the early days before report writing tools were available. In those days we had to measure every column of the page for every field. Talking to other professionals, this is a common problem with current non-static GUI tools.

Java packages

There are three main packages that hold the tools that you will need to build GUIs:

1. java.awt - the older Java graphics library. Still needed.
2. javax.swing The newer Java graphics library
3. java.awt.event – has the event classes you need for setting up event driven classes.

Java graphics are based around components. Containers are a subset of components that can hold other components.

Containers

The basic java container classes are:

- JWindow – A plain GUI screen
- JFrame – A child of JWindow That includes some basic window tools.
- JPanel – used within a JFrame
- JApplet – used with web browser applications.

We will concentrate our discussion on JFrame. However, JFrame has some (to me) significant limitations.

For instance, if you build the following code:

```
JFrame aFrame = new JFrame("Hello World");
```

And run it, nothing happens.

The default JFrame has no size and the initial setting is not visible.
You have to add the line:

```
aFrame.setVisible(true);
```

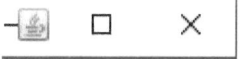

Now it is visible in the top right corner, but not very useful, since it has no size and when you click the x the program is still running in the background. You must hit ctrl c to stop it. in order to get it to quit. So, I wrote the CSCI class Frame2 to set the defaults to be visible and end the program when you close the GUI. It also sets an initial size of 500 x 500 pixels and centers the GUI on the screen.

Using Frame2 instead of JFrame. Our program testJFrame becomes testFrame2, we import CSCI and change the aFrame definition to become.

```
Frame2 aFrame = new Frame2("Hello World");
```

And when we click the z in the left-hand corner, the program terminates. This is our basic container. To make this program interesting, we need to add some component objects.

Component objects

To build an object takes at least two steps. Step one declares the object. Step two declares where the object belongs (what container owns it).

The simplest object is the label. Labels do nothing but display information. The java class is JLabel. To define the object

```
JLabel statement = new JLabel("HelloWorld);
```

To tell the object where it belongs we add it to the owner (sometimes called the parent (this is not inheritance).

```
aFrame.add(statement);
```

Our new program looks like:

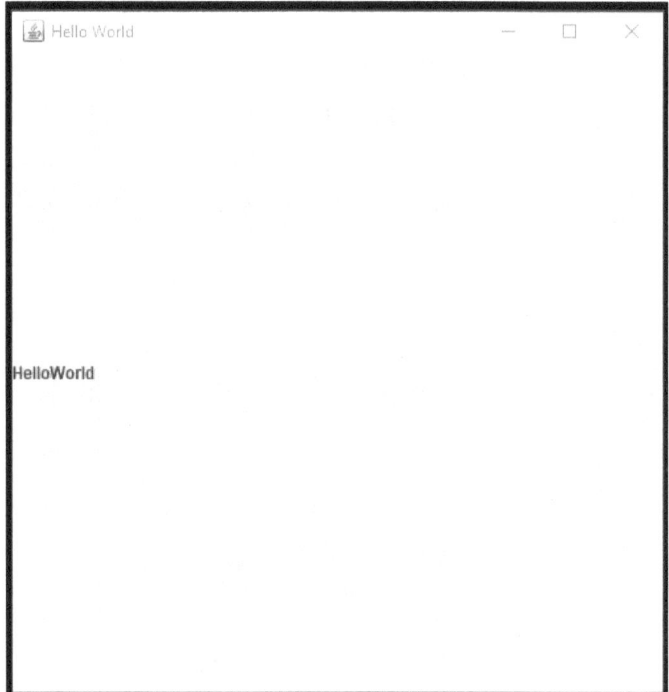

Not very attractive is it?

We could use the pack command after we have added our one item and make the frame smaller

```
aFrame.pack();
```

But this gives us a really small window:

As you can see, the pack method shrinks the container to the size of the objects that it holds.

We could also change size of the frame manually, but that is tedious and can lead to problems (especially as our GUI changes.) So, elook at layout managers.

Layout Managers

There are several awt and swing Layout managers:

- BorderLayout
- BoxLayout
- CardLayout
- FlowLayout
- GridBagLayout
- GridLayout
- GroupLayout
- SpringLayout

I have not tried all of them, but I have two that I like. Say we added six labels to our program.

Note: I built a label method that adds a border to the label and centers the label contents.

```
// This method builds a label with a black font centered.

public static JLabel buildLabel(String text){
        JLabel label = new JLabel(text);
        label.setForeground(Color.BLACK);
        label.setHorizontalAlignment(JLabel.CENTER);
        label.setBorder(BorderFactory.createLineBorder(Color.black));
        return label;
}
```

```
// build and add all of the labels.
JLabel statement1 = buildLabel("First");
aFrame.add(statement1);
JLabel statement2 = buildLabel("Second");
aFrame.add(statement2);
JLabel statement3 = buildLabel("Thrid");
aFrame.add(statement3);
JLabel statement4 = buildLabel("Fourth");
aFrame.add(statement4);
JLabel statement5 = buildLabel("Fifth");
aFrame.add(statement5);
JLabel statement6 = buildLabel("Sixth");
aFrame.add(statement6);
// pack the frame
aFrame.pack();
```

With no layout, only the last one is displayed:

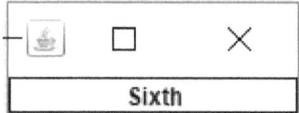

Shall we try a few layouts. With FlowLayout, no further information is required. Thus adding a single of code.

```
aFrame.setLayout(new FlowLayout());
```

And the result becomes:

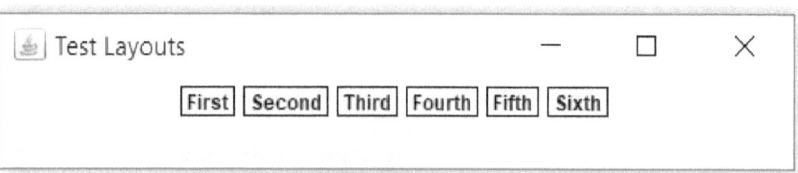

While readable, FlowLayout is rarely the result that we seek. This requires us to have our objects in order have our object in a horizontal line.

A nicer, though still restrictive layout manager is the BorderLayout . There are Five Areas (so we will skip our sixth label). When you add each object to the frame, you must specify the location that it goes in:

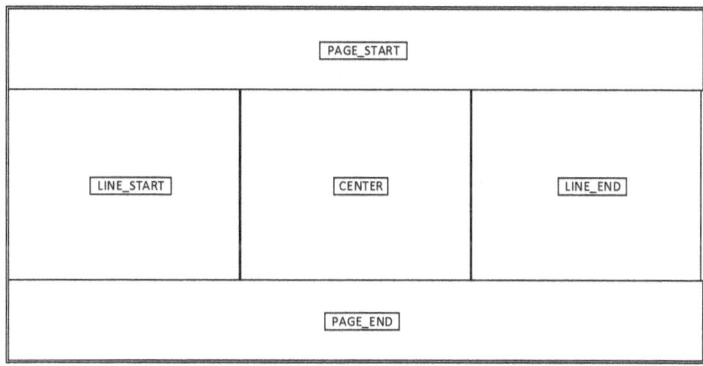

Each of these five areas so when you add them to the frame the add command becomes aframe.add(statement1, BorderLayout.PAGE_START)

So, the code for the border layout is

```
// add the labels
JLabel label1 = buildLabel(" First ");
aFrame.add(label1,BorderLayout.PAGE_START);
JLabel label2 = buildLabel(" Second ");
aFrame.add(label2,BorderLayout.LINE_START);
JLabel label3 = buildLabel(" Third ");
aFrame.add(label3,BorderLayout.CENTER);
JLabel label4 = buildLabel(" Fourth ");
aFrame.add(label4,BorderLayout.LINE_END);
JLabel label5 = buildLabel(" Fifth ");
aFrame.add(label5,BorderLayout.PAGE_END);
```

And gives us:

A prettier one (I think this is my favorite), but still easy is GridLayout. GridLayout lets you design a grid with as many evenly spaced rows and columns as you want. Since we have six labels. Let us try two, a 2 x 3 and a 3 x 2.

Like the FlowLayout objects land as you add them. You do not specify where they land.

So we replace the setLayout command with

```
aFrame.setLayout(new GridLayout(2,3));
```

And you end up with

First	Second	Third
Fourth	Fifth	Sixth

3x2

```
aFrame.setLayout(new GridLayout(3,2));
```

First	Second
Third	Fourth
Fifth	Sixth

Suppose you want to separate your screen into two or more parts or use two layout managers in one screen. Can you do this? Of Course, this is where the JPanel comes in.

JPanel

JPanel is a container that must be held in a separate container. So you can instantiate one or more JPanels and add them to a JFrame. You can then put different layout managers in each JPanel and add your objects to the JPanel. You can even add JPanels to a JPanel.

So, I defined my frame with a grid layout so that the two panels would lay side by side.:

283

```
// set up the frame.
Frame2 aFrame = new Frame2("Test Layouts");
aFrame.setSize(SIZE,SIZE);
aFrame.setLayout(new GridLayout(1,2));
```

I then defined my two panels with borders so I
could see them.

```
// set up the first panel panelA
JPanel panelA =
new JPanel();
panelA.setBorder(BorderFactory.createLineBorder(Color.black));
```

```
// set up the Second Panel panelB
JPanel panelB =
new JPanel();
panelB.setBorder(BorderFactory.createLineBorder(Color.black));

 aFrame.add(panelB);
```

I copied code from two of my previous programs.
I used the borderLayout for panel A and the 3x2
Grid for panel B. I changed the text in panel B.

```
// panelA will be a borderlayout with 5 labels.
panelA.setLayout(new BorderLayout());

// fill panelA

JLabel statement1 = buildLabel("First");
panelA.add(statement1,BorderLayout.PAGE_START);
JLabel statement2 = buildLabel("Second");
panelA.add(statement2,BorderLayout.LINE_START);
JLabel statement3 = buildLabel("Third");
panelA.add(statement3,BorderLayout.CENTER);
JLabel statement4 = buildLabel("Fourth");
panelA.add(statement4,BorderLayout.LINE_END);
JLabel statement5 = buildLabel("Fifth");
panelA.add(statement5,BorderLayout.PAGE_END);
```

```
// Panel B will be a Grid Layout with 6 labels.
// Fill PanelB

panelB.setLayout(new GridLayout(3,2));
JLabel label1 = buildLabel("once");
panelB.add(label1);
JLabel label2 = buildLabel("upon");
panelB.add(label2);
JLabel label3 = buildLabel("a");
panelB.add(label3);
JLabel label4 = buildLabel("midnight");
panelB.add(label4);
JLabel label5 = buildLabel("dreary");
panelB.add(label5);
JLabel label6 = buildLabel("sat");
panelB.add(label6);
```

And the output looks like

Once we can create a static GUI, now we need to
worry about an interactive GUI.

Interactive GUIs

The Event Driven model

Events remind me of the try{}catch{} error handling model that we discussed earlier. An Event such as a mouse click happens. A listener catches the event and then a handler takes action.

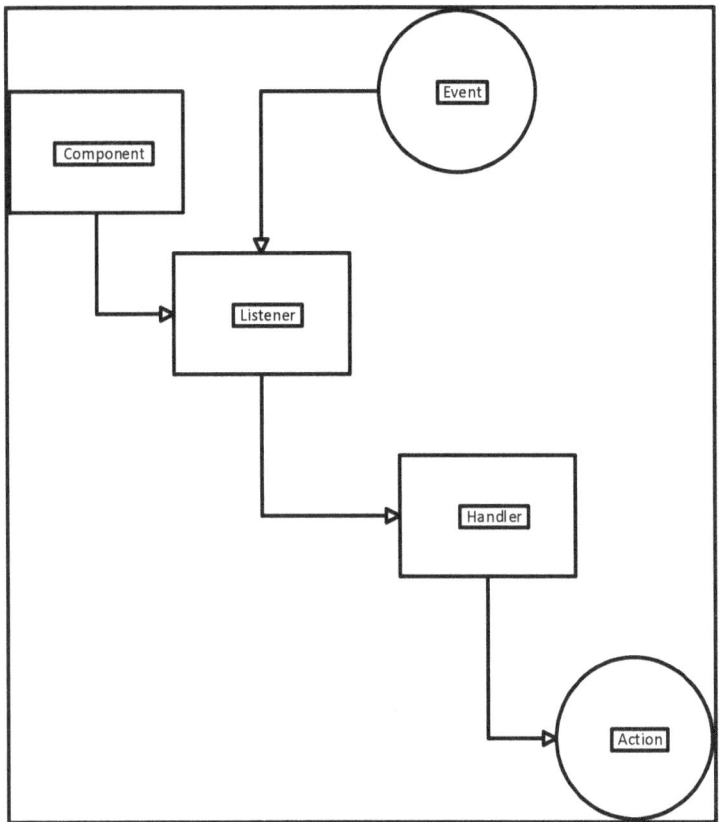

So you define your component you add the listener to the component, you define the event a class that implements the interface ActionListener and implemented the method actionPerformed(). Our class is our listener and actionPerformed() is the handler. Our first attempt is:

```
package GBlood;
import java.awt.event.*;
public class listener implements ActionListener{
public void actionPerformed(ActionEvent e){
        System.out.println("Button clicked ");
}
}
```

The driver is

```
static final int SIZE = 300;
public static void main (String[] args)
{
        listener buttonListener = new listener();
        Frame2 aFrame = new Frame2("Events");
        aFrame.setSize(SIZE,SIZE);
        aFrame.setLayout(new GridLayout(2,1));
        JLabel label = new JLabel("Press Button",JLabel.CENTER);
        aFrame.add(label);
        JButton button = new JButton("PUSH ME");
        aFrame.add(button);
        button.addActionListener(buttonListener);

}
```

This is not very satisfying. Basically, every time the button is clicked an output "Button clicked" is sent to standard output. Can we make improve our first attempt?

Remember our goal is to make this three tiered. We need to be able to have the handler talk to the GUI and the business Logic.

How do we improve our handler? Currently, we only handle one action. The button clicking. The action is controlled by the main program. If the main program added a second action, we would handle it in the precise same manner.

We are also going to be adding other components and wanting them to act in the same way, so this is the case where we may want to think of this in an abstract manner.

Every component can have an actionListener. So, if we build an abstract listener that leaves a way to get a String from the component (say an abstract method), we can build most of our code one time. So my abstractListener may look like:

```java
// constructor
public abstractPrintListener(String inSource){

        source = inSource;
}
// handler
public void actionPerformed(ActionEvent e){
        // Get the data from the source object
        // and send it down the pipe.
        Object comp = e.getSource();
        String line = getText(comp);
        System.out.println(source + ": " + line);
}
```

And each component type has to write its own

```java
// each source object will have its own way to get text.
// hence its own class
abstract public String getText(Object comp);
}
```

Which is very simple. You then create a listener object and add it each individual component. That object knows which component calls it.

For instance, the JButton listener, getText looks like:

```
public String getText(Object comp){
        //JButton's use getText.
        JButton button = (JButton) comp;
        String line = (String)button.getText();
        return line;
}
```

.

If we added a second button:

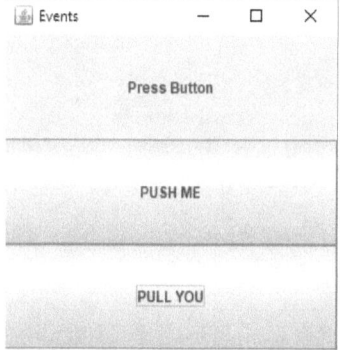

We simply add the listener to each button.

Now how do we share information between modules.

Remembering our discussion in the multitasking chapter, we had three main models. Shared memory, messaging, and pipes. Shared memory and messaging are synchronous, but pipes are asynchronous. Information in pipes can be picked up whenever they are desired. messaging is used whenever it is used. We want to be able to modify our memory and we want to use asynchronous communications, so pipes may be a good model. However, we want to update the GUI as soon as the process is finished so, let's use a GUI API to update the GUI. We can make the pushMePullYou a tad more interesting by allowing the buttons to change the label text. commActions is the business Logic that changes the label.

To do this we add in a pipe to the main program and make everything into threads. So, the main program becomes:

```
public static void main (String[] args)
{
    // set up the comm pipe
        commPipe guiComm = new commPipe();
        // start the GUI
        changeLabel GUI = new changeLabel(guiComm);
        // set up and start the business logic
        commActions actions = new commActions(guiComm,GUI);
        actions.start();

}
```

The single commPipe that we will use is guiComm. The listener will write to the pipe and the label writing class (commActions) will read from it.

The GUI changeLabel is the same as the previous GUI. We are changing the listener to use buttonListener that is a child of abstractCompListener instead of writing to standard out, it writes to the pipe guiComm

```
// handler
public void actionPerformed(ActionEvent e){
        // Get the data from the source object
        // and send it down the pipe.
        Object comp = e.getSource();
        String line = getText(comp);
        writer.write(source + ": " + line);
}
```

So the new business logic class commActions
reads from the guiComm pipe and executes our
new changelabel method updateLabel(). It gets
passed the GUI address from the main method.

```
public static void main (String[] args)
{

    // set up the comm pipe
        commPipe guiComm = new commPipe();
        // start the GUI
        changeLabel GUI = new changeLabel(guiComm);
        // set up and start the business logic
        commActions actions = new commActions(guiComm,GUI);
        actions.start();

}
```

This object reads the newText from the guicomm
Pipe and then updates the label.

All three of these tasks are working simultaneously
and asynchronously.

The GUI thread is running all of time displaying
the graphical window changing the window as
necessary.
The Listener thread is running waiting for an event
to happen, such as a button to press.
The actions thread is running waiting for a message
to appear in its pipe queue.

If a button is pressed (say PUSH ME).

The listener thread notes the event and kicks off the handler that then sends the appropriate message across the pipe.

The actions thread sees that there is a message on the pipe reads it and calls GUI.updateLabel to change the Label.

The GUI thread executes that method updates the label and refreshes the GUI screen.

And we end up with:

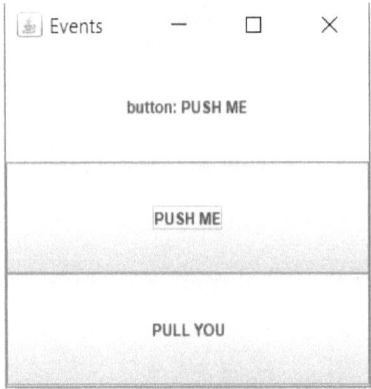

If we then press PULL YOU:

So, we have seen how a simple three-tier GUI program can work. Let us look at some of the tools that Java provides.

A complex multitiered GUI.

We build a simple main program to start the GUI and the business logic. It will also set up a commPipe to allow the GUI to talk to the business logic.

```
public static void main (String[] args)
{
    // set up the communication pipes
        commPipe guiComm = new commPipe();
        // set up the GUI threads
        compGUI GUI = new compGUI(guiComm);
        // set up the Action thread and start it.
        compActions actions = new compActions(guiComm,GUI);
        actions.start();
}
```

The best practice for a complex GUI is to have it in its own thread. However, the swing library is not thread-safe. Therefore, we use

javax.swing.SwingUtilities.invokeLater() to run the
GUI thread.

```
// this is the GUI thread
public void kickoff(){
        // We want to run the GUI this way
        // to avoid thread problems with the event driver.
        javax.swing.SwingUtilities.invokeLater(new Runnable()
            public void run() {
                    createAndShowGUI();
            }
        });
}
```

We will use the same business logic that we used
in the update label logic example.

Other Components

Java includes a great many built-in components
that you would recognize from various GUIs that
you have experienced in the past. We will look at
a few, you can explore more on your own. Besides
labels and buttons, some of the other most useful
components are:

Text Field (JTextField)
check boxes (JCheckBox)
radio buttons (JRadioBox)
combo boxes (JComboBox)

Like buttons, these must fit within a container.
we define our class variables, and kickoff the GUI
when the GUI is declared in the main.

```
public compGUI(commPipe tempComm){
    guiComm = tempComm;
        aFrame = new Frame2("Components");
        outcome = new JLabel("",JLabel.CENTER);
        kickoff();
}
```

We build our GUI in createAndShowGUI(), which
is run by kickoff(). We will start with a GUI
Frame.

```
// set up the frame.
aFrame.setSize(SIZE,SIZE);
aFrame.setLayout(new GridLayout(3,1));
```

We defined SIZE to be 300. This is large enough
for our components and small enough to show our
GUI in the book.

I chose a grid of 3 vertical panels. Because that fit
the components nicely.

Now we already defined the Label, so we setup the
Label Panel and add it to the aFrame first. This
puts it at the top.

```
JPanel panel1 = new JPanel();
panel1.setBackground(Color.WHITE);
panel1.setborder(
BorderFactory.createLineborder(Color.black)
panel1.add(outcome);
aFrame.add(panel1);
```

The method updateLabel() is the only way that this
label gets changed.

```
// this is the API to modify the label.
public   void updateLabel(String newText){
         outcome.setText(newText);
         outcome.setForeground(Color.BLACK);
         aFrame.repaint();
}
```

ActionListeners

All of the remaining objects that we will discuss
will require a Listener to be attached to it. It turns
out that actionListeners worked well for this
situation. We used the same abstractCompListener
as in the previous example and just built a child for
each component.

The event happens -> the listener picks up the
event -> activates the handler (actionPerformed) ->
the handler sends a message to the business logic.

Each child listener overrides getText() since that
will depend on the component's way of getting
information out.

 Let's look at the actual implementation of each
component.

Component implementation

Next we define the Text field (JTextField) and the
combo box (JCombobox) and put them next to
each other. We put these together in a JPane and
set these below the Label. You can write anything
in the Text field, and it will be displayed in the
label with a brief description of the source.

```
// first component is a text field that
// they can input any data in.
JTextField text = new JTextField("Change Me");
text.setBorder(BorderFactory.createLineBorder(Color.black));
docListener txtListener = new docListener("text",guiComm);
text.addActionListener(txtListener);
```

And getText()

```
public String getText(Object comp){
        //JTextField's use getText.
        JTextField field = (JTextField) comp;
        String line = field.getText();
        return line;
}
```

The Text field could be totally random, but we set
up the combo box with a selection of animals to
choose from. The first item will be blank.

```
// some random data to choose from.
// leave the zero option blank for the combo box.
String[] animals = {"","Bird", "Cat", "Dog", "Rabbit", "Pig" };
```

So, the combo box is built from animals. We force
it to start at the blank entry. And we set up the
combolistener.

```
// second component is a combobox that they get to chose from our animals
JComboBox  combobox = new JComboBox(animals);
combobox.setSelectedIndex(0);
combobox.setBorder(BorderFactory.createLineBorder(Color.black));
comboListener boxListener = new comboListener("animal combo", guiComm);
combobox.addActionListener(boxListener);
```

ComboListener.getText()

```
public String getText(Object comp){
        //JComboBox's use getSelectedItem()
        JComboBox combo = (JComboBox) comp;
        String line = (String)combo.getSelectedItem();
        return line;
}
```

Next, we build the textPanel with field and combo and add this panel to aFrame.

```
// these two componets are in our second JPanel
JPanel panel2 = new JPanel();
panel2.setLayout(new GridLayout(1,2));
panel2.setBorder(BorderFactory.createLineBorder(Color.black));
panel2.add(text);
panel2.add(combobox);
aFrame.add(panel2);
```

Radio buttons (JRadioButtons) are a tad more complicated. They are individual components. Therefore, you have to set up the listener for each radio button. I called this one radioListener. getText() is

```
public String getText(Object comp){
        //JRadioButton's use getText.
        JRadioButton button = (JRadioButton) comp;
        String line = (String)button.getText();
        return line;
}
```

Since I needed Six radio buttons, I decided to build an ArrayList and a method, buildRadioButtons() to create them.

```
ArrayList<JRadioButton> radioButtons =
buildradioButtons(animals,rbListener);
```

```
// This builds our radio buttons.
public ArrayList<JRadioButton> buildradioButtons(String[] input
, radioListener rbListener){
        int size = input.length - 1;
        JRadioButton anItem;
        ArrayList<JRadioButton> output =
        new ArrayList<JRadioButton>();
        for(int i = 0; i < size; ++ i){
                // don't add the blank animal to the list
                anItem = new JRadioButton(input[i+1]);
                anItem.addActionListener(rbListener);
                output.add(anItem);
        }

        return output;
}
```

You want these radio buttons to be implemented as a group. You want to implement radio buttons in such a way as to allow one and only one to be selected at a time. You need two tools to do this. One is a container JPanel. The other is called a ButtonGroup. A button group ensures that only one item is selected at time.

```
ButtonGroup radioGroup = new ButtonGroup();
buildRadioGroup(radioButtons,buttonPanel,radioGroup);
```

buildRadioGroup()

```
public void buildRadioGroup(ArrayList<JRadioButton> input
, JPanel outPanel, ButtonGroup outGroup){

        int size = input.size();
        JRadioButton anItem;
        for(int i = 0; i < size; ++ i){
                anItem = input.get(i);
                outPanel.add(anItem);
                outGroup.add(anItem);
        }
}
```

Check Box (JCheckBox). There are two ways to design a check box. One way allows the user to select any or all the items from a check box and when finished push a button to process the selections. The other treats check boxes like radio buttons and select one and only one item. I chose the latter implementation. Therefore, I built the same structures that I did for the radio buttons.

```
//build the checkbox
checkListener cListener = new checkListener("animal Check Box", guiComm);
ArrayList<JCheckBox> checkbox = buildCheckBoxes(animals,cListener );

JPanel checkPanel = new JPanel();
checkPanel.setLayout(new GridLayout(size,1));
checkPanel.setBorder(BorderFactory.createLineBorder(Color.black));
ButtonGroup checkGroup = new ButtonGroup();
buildCheckGroup(checkbox,checkPanel,checkGroup);
```

buildCheckBoxes() and buildCheckGroup() are almost identical to the methods built for the radio group.

The final step was to build a JPanel to hold these two buttonPanel and checkPanel and add it to the aFrame.

```
JPanel panel3 = new JPanel();
panel3.setLayout(new GridLayout(1,2));
panel3.setborder(
BorderFactory.createLineborder(Color.black)
panel3.add(buttonPanel);
panel3.add(checkPanel);
aFrame.add(panel3);
```

300

Our final GUI looks like:

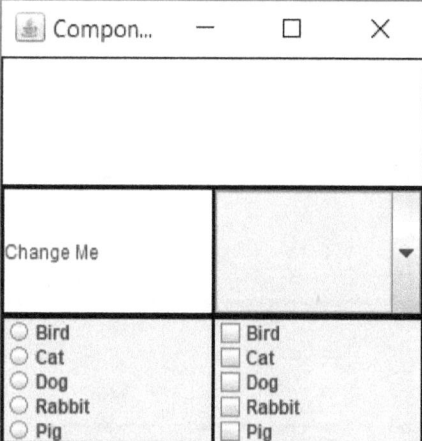

We change the Text field

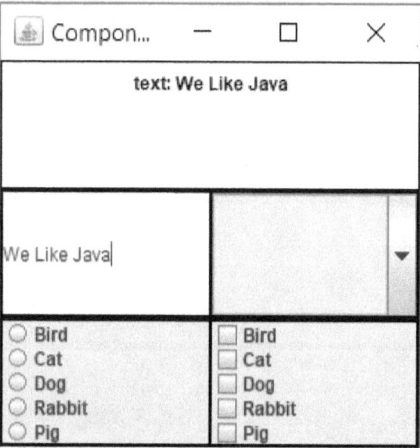

We select something from the combo box

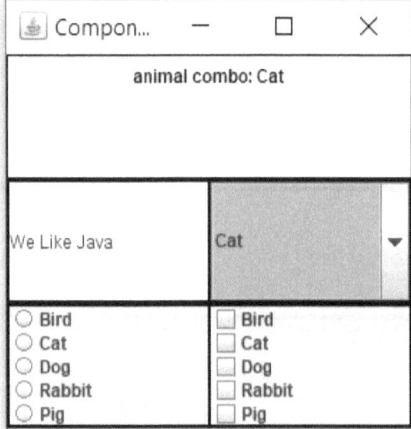

We choose a radio button:

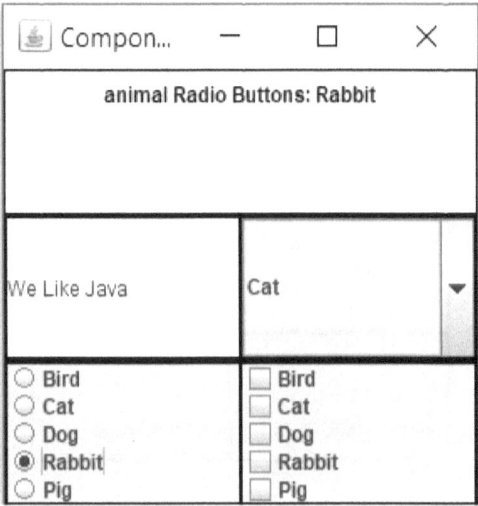

Finally, we select a check box

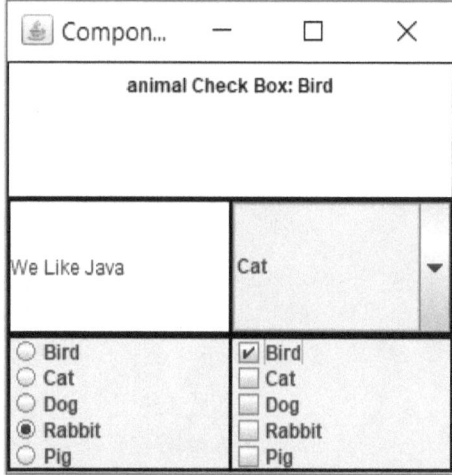

As you can see this boring GUI acts the way that we expect it to. The non-text fields do not allow us to select anything other than the allowed choices. Much like our non-GUI menus. Someone less-aesthetically challenged than me could create a much more beautiful GUI.

But this simple GUI is complicated. Although I am not an experienced GUI developer, and I am sure that I made many simplifications. I made it as maintainable as possible. However, there are a lot of moving parts. 15 Objects, 4 different listeners (based on 1 abstract listener), 5 panels. One Comm Pipe. One message (updateLabel()). The business logic is overly simplistic.

The bottom line that I would hope to get through to you is that GUI design is complex.
Implementation is tedious. Maintenance is scary.

Review

GUI Development is based on three Java packages

    javax.swing
    java.awt
    java.awt.evevnt

While you can build some simple GUIs using JOptionPane's methods, for more complex GUI's you are going to have to get comfortable using JFrames, JPanels, and other java components.

We explored some simple, stupid GUI's and developed a simple three-tiered parallel processing model using pipes, shared memory and an API call to display the usage of several components. We showed the progression of event processing.

An event happens -> a listener picks up the event -> listener calls the handler _> handler causes an action to occur.

We had the handler communicate to the business logic that then told the GUI what to do.

Javax.swing has more components than you will ever want to use. It will probably take a lifetime to become an expert at all of them. However, there are probably only a few that you will enjoy using. Mixing them up, like we did in our example is probably not the best practice.

Challenge

Suppose you wanted to build a tip calculator.

- You might have a text field (preferably a formatted text field) for entering the bill total.
- When enter is hit. A listener is picks up the eventListener activates handler that sends amount to tip amount calculator.
- Tip amount calculator calculates various tipe say (5%, 10%, 15%, 20%, 25%) and sends those back to GUI
- GUI displays tip option in second JPanel (say button Group).
- User selects tip. A listener is picks up the event
- Listener activates handler that sends Tip and Bill amount to final bill calculator.
- Final Bill calculator sends final amount back to GUI.
- GUI displays Final Amount.

So, your GUI needs 3 JPanels, 2 JLabels, 5 JButtons (maybe six if you want 0% tip), 1 ButtonGroup, 1 JFrame. 2 Listeners, 2 commPipes, and 2 Business Logics and 1 main.

It would use concepts from every chapter in this book. Do you think you could build it?

Questions

1. Java GUI is based on two types of things they are:
   a) Containers and components.
   b) Holders and holdees.
   c) Parents and children
   d) Frames and labels.
2. Java GUIs event processing is based on
   a) Event happens -> component acts.
   b) Event happens -> listener traps event -> calls event handler
   c) Event happens -> container traps event -> calls event handler.
   d) Event happens -> handler traps event -> calls event listener
3. Listeners are attached to:
   a) Methods
   b) Components
   c) Events
   d) Handlers
4. The default behavior of JFRAME is:
   a) Invisible and does not end the process on exit.
   b) Visible and does not end the process on exit.
   c) Visible and ends the process on exit.
   d) Invisible and ends the process on exit.
5. JPanels can be used to:
   a) Divide JFrames.
   b) Combine components.
   c) Format display.
   d) All of the above.
6. ButtonGroup is used to:
   a) Force buttons to line up nicely.
   b) Force some components to only select one at a time.
   c) Act as a JPanel in a JFrame.
   d) None of the above.

7. JOptionPane can be used to:
   a) Create simple GUIs.
   b) Set up options for JPanes.
   c) Build Complex GUIs without a lot of work.
   d) None of the above.
8. To attach a listener to a component, use the ___ command.
   a) add
   b) attach
   c) listen
   d) hear
9. To set up the 3-tier model, you place the business logic in:
   a) The GUI.
   b) The listener.
   c) The event handler.
   d) A separate process.
10. The main libraries for Java GUIs do not include:
    a) javax.swing
    b) java.awt
    c) java.gui
    d) java.awt.event

Appendix A Java Reserved Words

abstract
assert
boolean
break
byte
case
catch
char
class
const
continue
default
do
double
else
enum
extends
final
finally
float
for
goto
if
implements
import
instanceof
int
interface
long
native
new

package
private
protected
public
return
short
static
strictfp
super
switch
synchronized
this
throw
throws
transient
try
void
volatile
while

Appendix B CSCI Package.

The CSCI Package is a set of Utilities built to simplify coding in the CCGA courses. These utilities were designed to allow the students to code functionality before certain topics were presented and simplify their code.

To use the package:

Have the directory CSCI with all .java and/or .class files in your compilation directory.
You can compile the .java files by typing:

java CSCI*.java

include the statement

import CSCI.*;

before the class definition.

CSCI currently includes the following classes

- AgeUtility
- commPipe
- CSCIConvert
- CSCIMath
- DisplayTime
- FileIn
- FileOut
- Frame2
- Frequency
- FrequencySet
- keyBoard
- label
- Menu
- Person
- PersonRecord
- sharedCounter
- StringTools
- subFreq
- TitleMenu

Appendix C Resources

I made extensive use of the Oracle Documentation site to verify my concepts and Ideas.

http://docs.oracle.com/javase/8/docs

I learned Java from

Learning Java by Niemeyer and Leueck

I firmly believe that one of the finest books on Software engineering is

The Mythical Man Month by Frederick P. Brooks Jr.

I have used the following books in my classes over the past few years and concepts have affected this book:

Problem Solving and Programming Concepts by Mareen Sprangle and Jim Hubbard

Java Programming by Joyce Farrell

Over the past thirty some odd years, I have read more books and taken more courses than I can count or remember. All these courses and books have influenced this book to some degree or another.

Oracle Java JDK Download Site

www.oracle.com/technetwork/java/javase/downloads/index.html

Use this site to download the latest Java JDK. The JDK is the Development Kit. It has the necessary executables and support files for the java compiler and the virtual machine.

Warning: After you have run the JDK, you still may need to make sure that javac is part of your path in order to use it. Example: You may need to add C:\Program Files\Java\jdk1.8.0_65\bin to the Path Variable in your Environment Variables.

NotePad++ official Site

https://notepad-plus-plus.org/

This is the official site for the Notepad++ download and is a free download.

Appendix D Sample Standards

CSCI 1301 1302 Standards

Name your main class and file with the same name.
Name your main class First Initial Last Name Classname.
Example: Say the program name was RenameFiles, my main class would be GBloodRenameFiles
Use the program names specified in the assignments
Use the recommended designs.
Use good Software Engineering practices

1302 specific Standards

Name your package First Initial Last Name, mine is GBlood
Your main class goes in the default package all other class files go into your package.
Don't forget the appropriate package and import statements.
Use Inheritance and composition don't copy classes into your code.

Good Software Engineering Practices

Write Clean, simple code.
Comment your code.
Modularize your code. Use loose coupling and high cohesion between methods.
Be consistent in variable naming.
Use meaningful names.
Use char, double, int, and String data types.
Use verbs to name methods, nouns and adjectives for variables.
Never hard code file names or paths, use command line arguments, standard input, or a configuration file.
Reuse code, do not reinvent the wheel
Use CSCI classes don't copy them into your code.
Make sure that your code compiles successfully before you turn it in
Make sure that your code runs successfully before you turn it in
Check your code against reasonable test cases

10

Appendix E Vocabulary

Term	Definition
Algorithm	A solution to a problem that can be solved through a sequence of instructions.
Algorithmic solution	A sequence of instructions to solve a problem. A computer programmer writes a solution in the form of an algorithm before coding it into a computer language.
Array	Sometimes called a subscripted variable; a block of memory locations in the internal memory that is assigned to one variable name. Arrays may be one-dimensional, twodimensional, or multidimensional.
Assembly language	A three-letter representation of a machine language instruction.
Base-one system	A computer system in which array element numbers begin with one rather than zero.
Base-zero system	A computer system in which element numbers begin with zero rather than one.
Batch processing	Running successive sets of data through a program all at one time without human intervention.
Binary search	A technique used to search for a single element in an array or a single record in a file.
Bug	An error in a computer program.

Calculation module	A Process module that does arithmetic calculations and accumulates, counts, or manipulates numeric data in some way.
Case logic structure	One of the four logic structures for organizing the instructions to the computer that make up a program. The case structure allows the computer to select one set of instructions from among many, through data given by the user or calculated in the solution.
cast operator	an operator that performs an explicit type conversion; it is created by placing the desired result type in parentheses before the expression to be converted.
char	the data type that holds any single character.
character	any letter, number, or special symbol (such as a punctuation mark) that comprises data.
Character data	The data set of the character data type; it includes all symbols available on a computer.
catch	The block in the exception logic that handles the exception that is thrown by the try block.
Class	A class is part of a solution of an object-oriented solution to a problem. A class models the properties or characteristics of a set of objects.

class body	the set of data items and methods between the curly braces that follow the class header.
class definition	a description of attributes and methods of objects instantiated from a class. the top section contains the name of the class, the middle section contains the names and data types of the attributes, and the bottom section contains the methods.
Class diagram	A UML diagram that describes the structure of a system with its classes, attributes, and class relationships.
class methods	static methods that do not have a this reference (because they have no object associated with them).
class user	an application or class that instantiates objects of another prewritten class. See also class client.
class variables	static variables that are shared by every instantiation of a class.
close the file	to make a file no longer available to an application.
Cohesion	Concept that a method has one purpose and its independence from other methods.
collision	describes a class naming conflict.
Concatenation	Adding one piece of string data to another by placing the second piece immediately after the first.

Constant	A value in a program that cannot change during processing.
Control module	The module controlling the processing of all of the subtasks in a solution.
counting	the process of continually incrementing a variable to keep track of the number of occurrences of some event.
Coupling	Concept of how any two modules communicate with each other.
crash	a premature, unexpected, and inelegant end to a program.
Data	Unorganized facts.
data fields	data variables declared in a class outside of any method.
data files	files that consist of related records that contain facts and figures, such as employee numbers, names, and salaries.
data type	describes the type of data that can be stored in a variable, how much memory the item occupies, and what types of operations can be performed on the data.
Data type	The kind of data of a variable or a constant. The three basic data types are numeric, character, and logical.
Data Validation module	Module that Checks data to make sure it is correct
Database Management System (DBMS)	Software that stores large quantities of data, organizes data, and prints reports.

dead code	unreachable statements.
Debugging	The process of correcting errors in a computer program.
decimal numbering system	the numbering system based on 10 digits, 0 through 9, in which each column value is 10 times the value of the column to its right.
Decision logic structure	One of the four logic structures for organizing the instructions to the computer that make up a program. The decision structure selects one of two sets of instructions according to the resultant of a condition.
Decision table	A programming aid to writing decision instructions for the computer; it consists of a rectangular grid divided into four parts, which specifies all possible actions the computer could take for each possible set of conditions.
declaration	another name for a method header; also, the statement that assigns a data type and identifier to a variable.
decrementing	the act of subtracting 1 from a variable.
default constructor	a constructor that requires no arguments.
default package	the unnamed package in which a class is placed if no package is specified.

Default value	A value of a variable that is built into a program and that the computer automatically uses unless the value is changed by the user.
definite loop	a loop that executes a predetermined number of times; a counted loop. Contrast with indefinite loop.
descending order	the order of objects arranged from highest to lowest value. See also ascending order.
development environment	a set of tools that helps programmers by providing such features as displaying a language's keywords in color.
directories	elements in a storage organization hierarchy. See also folders.
do...while loop	a loop that executes a loop body at least one time; it checks the loop control variable at the bottom of the loop after one repetition has occurred.
documentation comments	comments that automatically generate well-formatted program documentation.
do-nothing loop	a loop that performs no actions other than looping.
double	a data type that can hold a floating-point value of up to 14 or 15 significant digits of accuracy. Contrast with float.
double-precision floating-point number	a type of value that is stored in a double.

dummy values	values the user enters that are not "real" data, but just signals to stop data entry.
Dynamic array	An array in which the maximum number of elements can change during processing.
dynamic method binding	the ability of an application to select the correct subclass method when the program executes. See also late method binding.
dynamically resizable	describes an object whose size can change during program execution.
echoing the input	the act of repeating the user's entry as output so the user can visually confirm the entry's accuracy.
element	one variable or object in an array.
else clause	the part of an if...else statement that executes when the evaluated Boolean expression is false.
else...if clause	a format used in nested if statements in which each instance of else and its subsequent if are placed on the same line.
empty body	a block with no statements in it.
empty statement	a statement that contains only a semicolon.
encapsulation	the act of hiding data and methods within an object.

EndOfFile (EOF)	The marker in a computer solution indicating that there are no more records to be processed.
Equation	A variable that is assigned the value of an expression, another variable, or a constant, as in A = 5 + B, A = B (where B is a variable), or A = 5, respectively.
equivalency operator	the operator composed of two equal signs that compares values and returns true if they are equal.
escape sequence	a sequence that begins with a backslash followed by a character; the pair frequently represents a nonprinting character.
event-driven program	a program in which the user might initiate any number of events in any order.
exception	in object-oriented terminology, an unexpected or error condition.
exception handling	an object-oriented technique for managing or resolving errors.
exception specification	the practice of using the keyword throws followed by an Exception type in the method header. An exception specification is required when a method throws a checked Exception that it will not catch but will be caught by a different method.
executing	the act of carrying out a program statement or program.

explicit conversion	the data type transformation caused by using a cast operator.
Expression	An operation or series of operations performed on variables or constants, as in 5 + B.
extended	describes classes that have descended from another class.
extends	a keyword used to achieve inheritance in Java.
External documentation	Instructions to the user in the form of manuals or other written documents.
FAQs	frequently asked questions.
fault-tolerant	describes applications that are designed so that they continue to operate, possibly at a reduced level, when some part of the system fails.
field	a data variable declared in a class outside of any method. In reference to storage, a group of characters that has some meaning.
File	A collection of related records.
final	the keyword that precedes named constants, that describes superclass methods that cannot be overridden in a subclass, and describes classes in which all methods are final.
finally block	a block of code that executes at the end of a try...catch sequence.

fixed method binding	the opposite of dynamic method binding; it occurs when a subclass method is selected while the program compiles rather than while it is running. See also static method binding.
flag	a variable that holds a value (often true or false) to indicate whether some condition has been met.
float	a data type that can hold a floating- point value of up to six or seven significant digits of accuracy. Contrast with double.
floating-point	describes a number that contains decimal positions.
floating-point division	the operation in which two values are divided and either or both are floating-point values.
flowchart	a tool that helps programmers plan a program's logic by writing the steps in diagram form, as a series of shapes connected by arrows.
flushing	an operation to clear bytes that have been sent to a buffer for output but that have not yet been output to a hardware device.
folders	elements in a storage organization hierarchy. See also directories.
for loop	a loop that can be used when a definite number of loop iterations is required.
foreach loop	the enhanced for loop.

formal parameters	the variables in a method declaration that accept the values from actual parameters. Contrast with actual parameters.
format string	in a printf() statement, a string of characters that includes optional text (that is displayed literally) and one or more format specifiers.
fragile	describes classes that are prone to errors.
fully qualified identifier	describes a filename that includes the entire hierarchy in which a class is stored.
fundamental classes	basic classes contained in the java.lang package that are automatically imported into every program. Contrast with optional classes.
garbage value	the unknown value stored in an uninitialized variable.
generic programming	a feature of languages that allows methods to be used safely with multiple data types.
Global variable	A variable that can be accessed by all modules below and in line (in the interactivity chart) with the module that declared the variable.
goes out of scope	describes what happens to a variable at the end of the block in which it is declared. Contrast with comes into scope.
graphical user interfaces (GUIs)	environments that allow users to interact with a program in a graphical environment.

GUI components	graphical user interface components, such as buttons and text fields, with which the user can interact.
hardware	the general term for computer equipment.
has-a relationship	a relationship based on composition.
hash code	a calculated number used to identify an object.
Hashing	A method of using a predefined algorithm to designate the record number for fast retrieval of a given record.
header	the first line of a method; its declaration.
Heuristic solution	A solution to a problem that cannot be solved through a single sequence of instructions.
hexadecimal numbering system	a numbering system based on 16 digits, 0 through F, in which each column represents a value 16 times higher than the column to its right.
Hierarchy	The order in which operations are performed for mathematical, relational, and logical operations.
high-level programming language	a language that uses a vocabulary of reasonable terms, such as read, write, or add, instead of referencing the sequences of on and off switches that perform these tasks. Contrast with low-level programming language.

HTML (Hypertext Markup Language)	a simple language used to create Web pages.
identifier	the name of a program component such as a class, object, or variable.
if clause	the part of an if. . .else statement that executes when the evaluated Boolean expression is true.
if...else statement	a statement that provides the mechanism to perform one action when a Boolean expression evaluates as true, and to perform a different action when a Boolean expression evaluates as false.
immutable	describes objects that cannot be changed.
implementation	the actions that execute within a method; the method body.
implementation hiding	a principle of object-oriented programming that describes the encapsulation of method details within a class.
implicit conversion	the automatic transformation of one data type to another. Also called promotion.
import statement	a Java statement that allows access to a built-in Java class that is contained in a package.

inclusion polymorphism	the situation in which a single method implementation can be used with a variety of related objects because they are objects of subclasses of the parameter type. See also pure polymorphism.
Incrementing	The process of counting on the computer by adding a number to a previous number. The instruction for incrementing by one is Counter = Counter + 1.
indefinite loop	a loop in which the final number of iterations is unknown. Contrast with definite loop.
index	a subscript.
Indicator	A value built into a solution by the programmer to redirect the flow of processing.
infinite loop	a loop that never ends.
Information	Organized facts.
information hiding	the object-oriented programming principle used when creating private access for data fields; a class's private data can be changed or manipulated only by a class's own methods, and not by methods that belong to other classes.
inheritance	a mechanism that enables one class to inherit, or assume, both the behavior and the attributes of another class.
initialization	the act of making an assignment at the time of variable declaration.

initialization list	a series of values provided for an array when it is declared.
Initialization module	The module containing all of the processing that has to be completed only once and at the beginning of the solution.
inner block	a block contained in an outer block.
inner classes	nested classes that require an instance. See also nonstatic member classes.
inner loop	a loop that is contained entirely within another loop.
insertion sort	a sorting algorithm that operates by comparing each list element with earlier ones and, if the element is out of order, opening a spot for it by moving all subsequent elements down the list.
instance	an existing object of a class.
instance methods	methods used with object instantiations. See also nonstatic methods.
instance variables	the data components of a class.
instantiation	the process of creating an object.
int	the data type used to declare variables and constants that store integers in the range of − 2,147,483,648 to +2,147,483,647.
integer	a whole number without decimal places.

integer division	the operation in which one integer value is divided by another; the result contains no fractional part.
Interactive processing	Processing that involves user intervention to enter new data as needed, usually at a keyboard.
interactive program	a program in which the user makes direct requests.
Interactivity chart	A chart, also called a structure chart, showing all of the subtasks, or modules, in a program.
interface	a construct similar to a class, except that all of its methods must be abstract and all of its data (if any) must be static final; it declares method headers, but not the instructions within those methods. Also used to describe the part of a method that a client sees and uses. it includes the method's return type, name, and arguments.
Internal documentation	Remarks within a computer solution to explain the processing.
interpreter	a program that translates language statements into machine code. An interpreter translates and executes one statement at a time. Contrast with compiler.
invoke	to call or execute a method.

is-a relationship	the relationship between an object and the class of which it is a member.
iteration	one loop execution. J
Java	an object-oriented programming language used both for general-purpose business applications and for interactive, World Wide Web-based Internet applications.
Java API	the application programming interface, a collection of information about how to use every prewritten Java class.
Java applications	stand-alone Java programs.
Java ARchive (JAR) file	a file that compresses the stored data.
Java interpreter	the program that checks bytecode and communicates with the operating system, executing the bytecode instructions line by line within the Java Virtual Machine.
Java Virtual Machine (JVM)	a hypothetical (software-based) computer on which Java runs.
java.lang	the package that is implicitly imported into every Java program and that contains the fundamental classes.
Javadoc	a documentation generator that creates Application Programming Interface (API) documentation in Hypertext Markup Language (HTML) format from Java source code.

Javadoc comment	a special form of block comment that provides a standard way to document Java code.
Javadoc tag	a keyword within a comment that the Javadoc tool can process.
JDK	the Java Standard Edition Development Kit.
Key	The field of the records that is used to order a file or search for a record.
key field	the field in a record that makes the record unique from all others.
keyboard buffer	a small area of memory where keystrokes are stored before they are retrieved into a program. Also called the type-ahead buffer.
keywords	the words that are part of a programming language.
late method binding	the ability of an application to select the correct subclass method when the program executes. See also dynamic method binding.
lexicographical comparison	a comparison based on the integer Unicode values of characters.
library of classes	a folder that provides a convenient grouping for classes.

line comments	comments that start with two forward slashes (//) and continue to the end of the current line. Line comments can appear on a line by themselves or at the end of a line following executable code. Contrast with block comments.
literal constant	a value that is taken literally at each use. See also unnamed constant.
literal string	a series of characters that appear exactly as entered. Any literal string in Java appears between double quotation marks.
local classes	nested classes that are local to a block of code.
local variable	a variable known only within the boundaries of a method.
Local variable	A variable accessed by the module that declared the variable. A single variable can be both local and global (see Chapter 4).
logic	describes the order of program statements that produce correct results.
logic error	a programming bug that allows a source program to be translated to an executable program successfully, but that produces incorrect results.

Logic structure	A structure for organizing the instructions to the computer that make up a program. There are four logic structures: the sequential structure, the decision structure, the loop structure, and the case structure.
logical AND operator	an operator used between Boolean expressions to determine whether both are true. The AND operator is written as two ampersands (&&).
Logical data	The data set consisting of True and False, used in making yes-and-no decisions.
Logical operator	An operator within an expression that uses logical data as operands and produces logical data as the resultant. The logical operators include NOT, AND, and OR.
logical OR operator	an operator used between Boolean expressions to determine whether either expression is true. The OR operator is written as two pipes (||).
long	the data type that holds very large integers, from − 9,223,372,036,854,775,808 to 9,223,372,036,854,775,807.
loop	a structure that allows repeated execution of a block of statements.

loop body	the block of statements that executes when the Boolean expression that controls the loop is true.
loop control variable	a variable whose value determines whether loop execution continues.
loop fusion	the technique of combining two loops into one.
Loop logic structure	One of the four logic structures for organizing the instructions to the computer that make up a program. The loop structure enables the computer to process the same set of instructions repeatedly.
lossless conversion	a data type conversion in which no data is lost.
lossy conversion	a data type conversion in which some data is lost.
low-level programming language	a language that corresponds closely to a computer processor's circuitry. Contrast with high-level programming language. Compare with machine language.
machine code	machine language.
Machine language	Instructions represented by zeros and ones.
Master file	The file in which all of the data needed for processing are kept current.

Mathematical operator	An operator that uses numeric data as its operands and produces numeric data as the resultant. The mathematical operators include - (subtraction), + (addition), * (multiplication), / (division), \ (integer division), % (modulo division), and ^ (power).
matrix	a two-dimensional array.
member-level Javadoc comments	Javadoc comments that describe the fields, methods, and constructors of a class.
menus	lists of user options.
method	a program module that contains a series of statements that carry out a task.
method body	the set of statements between curly braces that follow the method header and carry out the method's actions.
method header	the declaration or first line of a method that contains information about how other methods interact with it.
method's type	the method's return type.
mission critical	a term that describes any crucial process in an organization.
modulus operator	the percent sign; when it is used with two integers, the result is an integer with the value of the remainder after division takes place. Also called the remainder operator; sometimes called just mod.

Multidimensional array	A multidimensional block of elements with a single variable name. Each element is designated by element numbers representing row, column, page, and so on.
multiple inheritance	the capability to inherit from more than one class; Java does not support multiple inheritance.
multiply and assign operator	an operator that alters the value of the operand on the left by multiplying the operand on the right by it; it is composed of an asterisk and an equal sign.
mutator methods	methods that set field values.
named constant	a named memory location whose value cannot change during program execution.
NaN	a three-letter abbreviation for Not a Number.
nanosecond	one-billionth of a second.
nested	describes the relationship of statements, blocks, or classes when one contains the other.
nested classes	classes contained in other classes.
nested if statements	describes if statements when one is contained within the other.
Nested If/Then/Else	A type of decision structure that nests one If/Then/Else instruction within another.
new operator	an operator that allocates the memory needed to hold an object.

nonabstract method	a method that is inherited.
nonstatic member classes	nested classes that require an instance. See also inner classes.
nonstatic methods	methods used with object instantiations. See also instance methods.
nonvolatile storage	storage that does not require power to retain information. Contrast with volatile storage.
NOT operator (!)	the operator that negates the result of any Boolean expression.
null String	an empty String created by typing a set of quotes with nothing between them.
numeric constant	a number whose value is taken literally at each use.
Numeric data	The data type that includes all numbers, integers and real numbers, and is the only data type that can be used in calculations.
object	an instance of a class.
Object class	a class defined in the java.lang package that is imported automatically into every Java program; every Java class descends from the Object class.
Object-oriented programming (OOP)	A language that supports object-oriented principles; a strategy of program design in which the data parts are the principal items, instead of the process.

one-dimensional array	an array that contains one column of values and whose elements are accessed using a single subscript. See also single-dimensional array.
open a file	the action that creates an object and associates a stream of bytes with it.
operand	a value used in an arithmetic statement.
Operator	A sign or symbol in an expression or equation telling the computer how to process the data. The three types of operators are mathematical, relational, and logical.
operator precedence	the rules for the order in which parts of a mathematical expression are evaluated.
optional classes	classes that reside in packages that must be explicitly imported into programs. Contrast with fundamental classes.
out of bounds	describes a subscript that is not within the allowed range for an array.
outer block	a block that contains a nested block.
outer loop	a loop that contains another loop.
overloading	describes using one term to indicate diverse meanings, or writing multiple methods with the same name but with different arguments.

override	to use the child class's version of a field or method instead of the parent's.
override annotation	a directive that notifies the compiler of the programmer's intention to override a parent class method in a child class.
package	a named collection or library of classes. See also library of classes.
Parallel arrays	Two or more arrays in which the data in the same element numbers are related to each other.
Parameter	A variable passed from one module to another module through the calling sequence of the module or function. There are two types of parameters, call-by-value parameters and call-by-reference. Call-by-value parameters cannot be changed in the module. Call-by-reference parameters can be changed and the changed value will be passed back to the calling module.
parent class	a base class.
Parsing	the process of breaking something into its component parts.
passed by reference	describes what happens when a reference (address) is passed to a method. Contrast with passed by value.

passed by value	describes what happens when a variable is passed to a method and a copy is made in the receiving method. Contrast with passed by reference.
passing arguments	the act of sending arguments to a method.
path	the complete list of the disk drive plus the hierarchy of directories in which a file resides.
path delimiter	the character used to separate path components.
pattern String	an argument composed of symbols that determine what a formatted number looks like.
permanent storage devices	hardware storage devices that retain data even when power is lost.
Pointer technique	A programming technique that uses the value in one array to point to an element in another array.
Polymorphism	The ability of an object of various types to respond to method call of the same name and act appropriately.
populating an array	the act of providing values for all of the elements in an array.
Positive logic	A type of decision logic in which the action the computer is to perform follows from the True side of the instruction.

postfix ++ or the postfix increment operator	an operator that is composed by placing two plus signs to the right of a variable; it evaluates the variable, then adds 1 to it. Contrast with prefix ++.
posttest loop	a loop in which the loop control variable is tested after the loop body executes. Contrast with pretest loop.
preferred size	a Component's default size.
prefix ++ or the prefix increment operator	an operator that is composed by placing two plus signs to the left of a variable; it adds 1 to the variable, then evaluates it. Contrast with postfix ++.
prefix and postfix decrement operators	operators that subtract 1 from a variable before and after evaluating it, respectively.
pretest loop	a loop in which the loop control variable is tested before the loop body executes. Contrast with posttest loop.
Primary key	A unique key that is the major key for ordering a file or searching for a record.
priming read or priming input	the first input statement prior to a loop that will execute subsequent input statements for the same variable.
primitive type	a simple data type. Java's primitive types are byte, short, int, long, float, double, char, and boolean.
Print module	A process module that prints the results of processing.
private access	describes a field or method that no other classes can access.

procedural programming	a style of programming in which sets of operations are executed one after another in sequence. Contrast with object-oriented programming.
procedures	sets of operations performed by a computer program.
Process modules	The modules that process the data. They include Calculation, Print, Read, and Data Validation modules.
Program	A computer solution to a problem; a set of instructions in a given computer language that solves the problem.
program comments	nonexecuting statements added to a Java file for the purpose of documentation.
program files	files that store software instructions.
program statements	similar to English sentences; they carry out the tasks that programs perform.
programmer-defined data type	a type that is created by a programmer and not built into the language; a class.
promotion	an implicit conversion.
prompt	a message that requests and describes user input.
property	an instance variable, field, or attribute of a class.

protected access	describes an intermediate level of security between public and private; a class's protected members can be used by a class and its descendants, but not by outside classes.
pseudocode	a tool that helps programmers plan a program's logic by writing plain English statements.
pseudorandom	describes numbers that appear to be random, but are the same set of numbers whenever the seed is the same.
public access	describes a field or method that outside classes can access.
pure polymorphism	the situation in which a single method implementation can be used with a variety of related objects because they are objects of subclasses of the parameter type. See also inclusion polymorphism.
Pushing and popping the stack	Adding (pushing) and taking from (popping) a stack.
Queue	A list in which the next value used was the first one to be added. Data are added and used in a first-in, first-out basis.
ragged array	a two-dimensional array that has rows of different lengths.
random access memory (RAM)	temporary, volatile storage.
random number	a number whose value cannot be predicted.

range check	a series of statements that determine within which of a set of ranges a value falls.
range match	the process of comparing a value to the endpoints of numerical ranges to find a category in which the value belongs.
Read module	A Process module that enters data into the computer.
Record	The set of data for one entity in a file or table.
Recursion	Recursion occurs when a module or a function calls itself.
redeclare a variable	to attempt to declare a variable twice. an illegal action.
reference	a variable that holds a memory address.
reference types	data types that hold memory addresses where values are stored.
Register	A high-speed temporary holding area built into the computer to hold instructions and data needed for the current processing.
Relational operator	An operator within an expression or equation that uses numeric or string data as operands and produces logical data as the resultant. The relational operators include: = (equal to), < (less than), > (greater than), <= (less than or equal to), >= (greater than or equal to), and < > (not equal to).

relative path	a path that depends on other path information to be complete.
remainder and assign operator	an operator that alters the value of the operand on the left by assigning the remainder when the left operand is divided by the right operand; it is composed of a percent sign and an equal sign (%=).
remainder operator	the percent sign; when it is used with two integers, the result is an integer with the value of the remainder after division takes place. Also called the modulus operator.
Report	A formatted output from a program.
Results	The required answers to or output from a problem.
return a value	to send a data value from a called method back to the calling method.
return statement	a statement that ends a method, and frequently sends a value from a called method back to the calling method.
return type	the type of data that, upon completion of a method, is sent back to its calling method.
robustness	describes the degree to which a system is resilient to stress, maintaining correct functioning.
root directory	the main directory of a storage device, outside any folders.

runtime error	an error that occurs when a program compiles successfully but does not execute.
runtime exceptions	unplanned exceptions that occur during a program's execution. The term is also used more specifically to describe members of the RuntimeException class.
scalar	describes simple, primitive variables, such as int, double, or char.
scientific notation	a display format that more conveniently expresses large or small numeric values; a multidigit number is converted to a single-digit number and multiplied by 10 to a power.
scope	the part of a program in which a variable exists and can be accessed using its unqualified name.
scope level	in Java, a variable's block. See also scope.
SDK	a software development kit, or a set of tools useful to programmers; the Java EE Development Kit.
searching an array	the process of comparing a value to a list of values in an array, looking for a match.
Secondary key	A key, which may or may not be unique, that is used to order a file or to search for one or more records in a file. A secondary key is considered a minor key.
seed	a starting value.

seekable	describes a file channel in which operations can start at any specified position.
semantic errors	the type of errors that occur when a correct word is used in the wrong context in program code.
sentinel	a value that stops a loop.
sequence structure	a logical structure in which one step follows another unconditionally.
sequential access file	a data file that contains records that are accessed one after the other in the order in which they were stored.
Sequential logic structure	One of the four logic structures for organizing the instructions to the computer that make up a solution. The sequential structure processes the instructions one after another in a sequence.
Sequential search	A method for locating a record in a file in which the computer starts at the first record and continues through the file, record by record, until the needed record is found.
shadowing	the action that occurs when a local variable hides a variable with the same name that is further away in scope.
short	the data type that holds small integers, from −32,768 to 32,767.

short-circuit evaluation	describes the feature of the AND and OR operators in which evaluation is performed only as far as necessary to make a final decision.
side effect	any action in a method other than returning a value.
signature	a method's name and the number, types, and order of arguments.
significant digits	refers to the mathematical accuracy of a value.
single-alternative selection	a decision structure that performs an action, or not, based on one alternative.
single-dimensional array	an array that contains one column of values and whose elements are accessed using a single subscript. See also one-dimensional array.
single-precision floating-point number	a type of value that is stored in a float.
software	the general term for computer programs.
Solution	The set of instructions to the computer that will output the results; a computer program before it is coded into a computer language.
Sorting	Arranging data in order; the order may be numeric or alphabetical.
source code	programming statements written in a high-level programming language.

Stack	A list in which the value to be added and the value to be used are on the same end of the list. Data are added and used in a last-in, first-out basis.
stack trace history list, or more simply stack trace	a list that displays all the methods that were called during program execution.
standard arithmetic operators	operators that are used to perform common calculations.
standard input device	normally the keyboard.
standard output device	normally the monitor.
state	the values of the attributes of an object.
static	a keyword that means a method is accessible and usable even though no objects of the class exist.
Static array	An array in which the maximum number of elements cannot change during processing.
static import feature	a feature in Java that allows you to use static constants without their class name.
static member class	a type of nested class that has access to all static methods of its top-level class.
Static method	A method that does not require an object to exist.

static method binding	the opposite of dynamic method binding; it occurs when a subclass method is selected while the program compiles rather than while it is running. See also fixed method binding.
Straight-through logic	A type of decision logic that processes all decisions sequentially, one after another.
stream	a pipeline or channel through which bytes flow into and out of an application.
String class	a class used to work with fixed-string data that is, unchanging data composed of multiple characters.
String variable	a named object of the String class.
strongly typed language	a language in which all variables must be declared before they can be used.
Structure chart	A chart, also called an interactivity chart, showing all of the subtasks, or modules, in a program.
stub	a method that contains no statements; programmers create stubs as temporary placeholders during the program development process.
subclass	a derived class.
subscript	an integer contained within square brackets that indicates one of an array's variables, or elements.

subtract and assign operator	an operator that alters the value of the operand on the left by subtracting the operand on the right from it; it is composed of a minus sign and an equal sign (− =).
subtype polymorphism	the ability of one method name to work appropriately for different subclasses of a parent class.
super	a Java keyword that always refers to a class's immediate superclass.
superclass	a base class.
switch statement	a statement that uses up to four keywords to test a single variable against a series of exact integer or character values. The keywords are switch, case, break, and default.
symbolic constant	a named constant.
syntactic salt	describes a language feature designed to make it harder to write bad code.
syntactic sugar	describes aspects of a computer language that make it "sweeter," or easier, for programmers to use.
Syntax	The rules of setting up instructions and commands in an operating system, a programming language, or an application program.

syntax error	a programming error that occurs when a program contains typing errors or incorrect language use; a program containing syntax errors cannot be translated into an executable program.
system software	the set of programs that manage the computer. Contrast with application software.
table	a two-dimensional array; a matrix. ternary operator an operator that needs three operands.
Term	Definition
text files	files that contain data that can be read in a text editor because the data has been encoded using a scheme such as ASCII or Unicode.
this reference	a reference to an object that is passed to any object's nonstatic class method.
threads of execution	units of processing that are scheduled by an operating system and that can be used to create multiple paths of control during program execution.
throw statement	a statement that sends an Exception out of a block or a method so it can be handled elsewhere.
throws clause	an exception specification in a method header.
TOCTTOU bug	an acronym that describes an error that occurs when changes take place from Time Of Check To Time Of Use.

token	a unit of data; the Scanner class separates input into tokens.
top-level class	the containing class in nested classes.
Traversal	Methods of accessing data within a tree structure.
try block	a block of code that a programmer acknowledges might generate an exception.
two-dimensional array	an array that contains two or more columns of values and whose elements are accessed using multiple subscripts. Contrast with one- dimensional array.
type casting	an action that forces a value of one data type to be used as a value of another type.
type conversion	the process of converting one data type to another.
type-ahead buffer	the keyboard buffer.
type-safe	describes a data type for which only appropriate behaviors are allowed.
type-wrapper classes	a method that can process primitive type values.
unary cast operator	a more complete name for the cast operator that performs explicit conversions.
unary operator	an operator that uses only one operand.
unchecked exceptions	exceptions that cannot reasonably be expected to be recovered from while a program is executing. Contrast with checked exceptions.

Unicode	an international system of character representation.
Unified Modeling Language (UML)	a graphical language used by programmers and analysts to describe classes and object-oriented processes.
unifying type	a single data type to which all operands in an expression are converted.
uninitialized variable	a variable that has been declared but that has not been assigned a value.
unnamed constant	a constant value that has no identifier associated with it. See also literal constant.
unreachable statements	statements that cannot be executed because the logical path can never encounter them; in some languages, including Java, an unreachable statement causes a compiler error. See also dead code.
upcast	to change an object to an object of a class higher in its inheritance hierarchy.
validating data	the process of ensuring that a value falls within a specified range.
variable	a named memory location whose contents can be altered during program execution.
variable declaration	a statement that reserves a named memory location.
virtual classes	the name given to abstract classes in some other programming languages, such as C++.

virtual key codes	codes that represent keyboard keys that have been pressed.
virtual keyboard	a computer keyboard that appears on the screen. A user operates it by using a mouse to point to and click keys; if the computer has a touch screen, the user touches keys with a finger or stylus.
virtual method calls	method calls in which the method used is determined when the program runs, because the type of the object used might not be known until the method executes.
void	a keyword that, when used in a method header, indicates that the method does not return any value when it is called.
volatile storage	memory that requires power to retain information. Contrast with nonvolatile storage.
while loop	a construct that executes a body of statements continually as long as the Boolean expression that controls entry into the loop continues to be true.
whitespace	any combination of nonprinting characters; for example, spaces, tabs, and carriage returns (blank lines).
wildcard symbol	a symbol used to indicate that it can be replaced by any set of characters. In a Java import statement, the wildcard symbol is an asterisk.

wrapped	to be encompassed in another type.
wrapper	a class or object that is "wrapped around" a simpler element.

www.ingramcontent.com/pod-product-compliance
Lightning Source LLC
Chambersburg PA
CBHW020724180526
45163CB00001B/93